Government Houses: Vice-Regal Residences of the Crown

First published in the United Kingdom in 2020.

ISBN: 978-1-5272-5980-5

Acknowledgements for referenced work is provided on page 176.

Book design and layout by Jeffrey Hyland.
Proofing and editing by Helen Cumberbatch.

Printed in the United Kingdom. Digital e-book also available.

For more information visit www.jeffreyhyland.wordpress.com/books.

GOVERNMENT HOUSES: VICE-REGAL RESIDENCES OF THE CROWN

JEFFREY HYLAND

GOVERNMENT HOUSES: VICE-REGAL RESIDENCES OF THE CROWN

Government Houses: An Introduction

This book brings together the history of the many current Vice-Regal residences across the Commonwealth and their relationships with the Royal Family over the years. Over the history of the British Empire initially, and later of the Commonwealth, the official residences of the sovereign's representative in many countries, territories, states and provinces came to be known as 'Government House'. One of the earliest references to Government House is said to date from India in 1845, however the term was in use before this. Originally, the title represented the centre of the administrative life of an overseas territory of the British Empire and the name came to personify both the Executive and Government of the territory. This was usually centred on a single building that housed the 'official life' of the territory that became known as Government House.

As many countries and territories began to establish separate Executives and Legislatures in national and state Parliaments and in Government administration buildings, Government House evolved to represent the place where the sovereign's representative would reside. These official residences were occupied by the resident Viceroy, Governor, Lieutenant-Governor, Commissioner or Administrator and later, following independence, by the Governor-General. These Government Houses also played host to the monarch and members of the Royal Family when they visited.

Some official residences were known as the Governor's House or even by different names linked to the location of the house or a local place name. In the United States, some formal dwellings of the Governor were known as Executive Mansions. However, the name of Government House came to be widely adopted across both the British Empire and the Commonwealth. In the late 19th century, the use of Government House was so widespread that Queen Victoria criticised Lady Stanley, the wife of the Governor-General of Canada, for heading her letters as written from Rideau Hall, the name still used today by the senior official Vice-Regal residence in Ottawa.

Jeffrey Hyland

Queen Victoria directed that Lady Stanley should refer to the residence as Government House, Canada.

The growth of the British Empire across the world meant that Government Houses were found in many faraway places from Canada to the Caribbean, from Africa to Asia and from Australia to the Pacific Ocean. At the height of the British Empire at the end of the 19th century, there were well over 120 Government Houses in all four corners of the world. These official residences and their occupants were in constant contact with the monarch through the British Foreign and Colonial Office as well as via written despatches sent to Buckingham Palace to keep the sovereign up to date with what was happening in their realms and territories.

During the 20th century, the British Empire became the Commonwealth of Nations and numerous countries and territories became independent. In many cases, the former Government House became known as 'State House' or the 'President's House' as new heads of state were elected and these official residences underwent a transition, as the country moved from monarchy to republic, although many countries also remained members of the Commonwealth. A number of these previous Vice-Regal residences retain traces of their historical past and the time when they were Government Houses of the Crown, although some properties have disappeared altogether and others have been adopted for different purposes.

Currently, there are around 50 remaining current Government Houses of the Commonwealth and this book explores their distinctive stories. Many of them are not the first Government House to occupy their place as the official building of the Crown in their respective country or territory. Government Houses can be found today in the Crown Dependencies, the British Overseas Territories and the Commonwealth realms of the Crown. In both Australia and Canada, the Vice-Regal residences extend to state and provincial level, where the monarch is represented by a State Governor or Lieutenant-Governor.

Many of these buildings are heritage sites that face constant maintenance challenges, often in very harsh climates, while still retaining their prestige and uniqueness. Yet at the same time, they are all at the centre of their nation, territory, province or state's official life and are members of a group of unique residences in the world.

Government Houses: An Introduction

The Royal Family and Government Houses

The role of Government House as the monarch's official residence was seen as immensely important and for the Vice-Regal residences to welcome the monarch or a member of the Royal Family was seen as a huge honour. It is largely recognised that the major growth and influence of the British Empire took place during the long reign of Queen Victoria from 1837 until 1901. Although Queen Victoria did not have the opportunity to visit the four corners of her vast Empire during her own lifetime, members of her family were able to travel to many countries and territories and frequently went to the many Government Houses that were being established.

Queen Victoria's father, Prince Edward, Duke of Kent and Strathearn, was the first member of the Royal Family to stay in North America for more than a short visit when he went to Nova Scotia and Québec between 1791 and 1793 to serve with the British Army. After spending time with the Army in the Caribbean, he returned to Canada for another two years before going back to England. He went to Canada again in 1799 as the newly appointed Commander-in-Chief of the British Forces in the Maritime Provinces of North America and remained for just over a year. He stayed at several Government Houses in Canada during his various times in North America, although they were not considered to be his official residence.

It is said that Prince Edward was the first person to use the term 'Canadian' in 1792 to refer to the French and British settlers living in what would come to be known as Upper and Lower Canada. The Prince would be permanently commemorated when the Legislature of St John's Island voted to change its name to Prince Edward Island in his honour in 1798, coming into effect the following year.

On his return from Canada, Prince Edward was widely expected to become the next Lord-Lieutenant of Ireland, however his next appointment was as the Governor of Gibraltar in March 1802. The Prince took up the role in May 1802, occupying Government House in Gibraltar, also known as The Convent, but his time there was short-lived and his harsh discipline resulted in a mutiny by the local troops. The Duke of Kent and Strathearn was recalled to London and he initially refused to leave the territory. He was denied permission to return to the territory but was allowed to keep the title of Governor of Gibraltar until his death in 1820 and the British outpost was governed by acting Governors in his place.

Queen Victoria took a great interest in her realms and territories, and so sent her children in her father's footsteps to undertake extensive royal tours of the British Empire on her behalf. Such visits in the late 19th and early 20th centuries, before the advent of air travel, would be long undertakings, involving several months away and arduous journeys by rail and sea. The respite that Government House could offer to the weary royal traveller was much welcomed.

Prince Albert Edward, the Prince of Wales, was sent on two long tours – to Canada and the United States in 1860 and to India in 1875–76 – when he stayed at many Government Houses and was received with great ceremony as the heir to the throne. Ostensibly these royal tours were designed to keep the mischievous Prince out of trouble, but they also served a greater purpose of connecting the British Empire to the monarch, and when royalty came to town, everyone wanted to be involved.

In Canada, the 18-year-old Prince of Wales arrived in Newfoundland on 23 July 1860, the first heir to the throne to cross the Atlantic Ocean, to begin a long tour of processions, banquets, receptions, levees and military parades in Nova Scotia, Prince Edward Island, Québec and Ontario. The Prince opened the great railway bridge across the St Lawrence River at Montréal and went on to lay the foundation stone for the new parliament building in Ottawa. His itinerary took him to Niagara Falls on the Canadian-US border, before he paid what was considered to be a private visit to the United States, although he was received by President James Buchanan at the White House.

Right: Statue of Queen Victoria in front of the National Library in Republic Square, Valletta, Malta. There are estimated to be over 150 major statues of Queen Victoria across the world, more than any other monarch in history.

The tour of India came at the request of Benjamin Disraeli's government, who wanted to show that Queen Victoria's interest in her Indian subjects was genuine and that it should be demonstrated through a royal visit. The tour was preceded by some controversy over who would be responsible for its cost and whether the Prince of Wales, who had no official position in public life at the time, took precedence over the Viceroy of India, who was the sovereign's representative. Subsequently, it was decided that the Prince would visit as the guest of the Viceroy and the question of precedence was largely avoided. The Prince of Wales and his very large entourage arrived in India on 8 November 1875, following visits to

The Royal Family and Government Houses

Greece, Egypt and Aden en route. His first port of call in India was Bombay (now Mumbai) where he stayed at the lavish Government House there at the invitation of the Governor, Sir Philip Wodehouse, and where the Prince's 34th birthday was celebrated with a grand party the next day. This Government House in Bombay, known as *Raj Bhavan* in India, was located in the suburb of Parel before the residence was moved to Malabar Point in 1883. The Prince of Wales would continue on his lengthy tour across India, Ceylon (now Sri Lanka) and Nepal, and he would stay in many official residences including spending Christmas with the Viceroy, Lord Northbrook, at his home and estate, named Belvedere House in Calcutta (now Kolkata in West Bengal). On his return to England via Egypt, Malta and Gibraltar – as well as to Spain and Portugal to visit King Alfonso XII of Spain and King Luis I of Portugal – the Prince expressed his delight at the success of the tour, and the relationship between the Princes of India and the Royal Family was certainly strengthened.

Queen Victoria's second son, Prince Alfred, Duke of Edinburgh, undertook his military training with the Royal Navy and, on completion, he was appointed as a midshipman on the HMS *Euryalus* at the age of 14. Two years later, in 1860, he paid an official visit to the Cape Colony (later to become South Africa) on the same ship. The young Prince came ashore to visit Government House in South Africa and was said to have made an impression on the locals. It was his first visit to a distant part of the British Empire and gave him a taste for overseas travel. In 1867, while in command of the frigate HMS *Galatea*, Prince Alfred became the first member of the Royal Family to visit Australia, arriving on 31 October in Glenelg, near Adelaide, South Australia. The Prince was received with huge interest and during his five-month visit and he visited the states of South Australia, Victoria, New South Wales, Queensland and Tasmania, often being entertained at the many Government Houses by the local Vice-Regal representative. Several institutions and buildings were named in his honour, including Prince Alfred College in Adelaide and the Royal Prince Alfred Hospital in Sydney.

Unfortunately, not everyone received the Prince's visit with such enthusiasm and he faced an assassination attempt in Sydney during a visit to the beachside suburb of Clontarf in March 1868. The Prince was shot in the back by an Irishman named Henry O'Farrell and, although seriously injured, he recovered thanks to several nurses, who had been trained under Florence Nightingale and had recently arrived in Australia. The experience did not deter Prince Alfred from his travels and just a year later, in 1869, he again undertook a long tour of Asia and the Pacific, becoming the first member of the Royal Family to visit New Zealand, staying at Government House in Auckland. He also went to Hawaii, Japan, India and Ceylon.

Below: An engraving showing the Royal Navy ship HMS *Euryalus* entering Simon's Bay near Cape Town in South Africa, circa 1860, which brought the young Prince Alfred, Duke of Edinburgh, on his first official visit overseas.

The Picture Art Collection/Alamy MW18XH

Right: Princess Louise stayed at several Government Houses in Canada in the 1870s and 1880s when her husband, John, Marquess of Lorne (later 9th Duke of Argyll), took up the post of Governor-General of Canada.

Following his marriage in 1874 to the Grand Duchess Maria Alexandrovna of Russia, the sixth child of Emperor Alexander II of Russia, in St Petersburg, Prince Alfred was stationed in Malta with his family as the Commander of the Mediterranean Fleet with the Royal Navy. His third child, Princess Victoria Melita, was born at Government House in Malta in 1876, which was for a time the family's residence as well as the home of the Governor of Malta, thus giving Princess Victoria Melita the unique distinction of being the only royal child to be born at a Government House. Today, Government House in Malta is the beautiful San Anton Palace, the official residence of the President of Malta, and it has played host to Queen Elizabeth II several times when she stayed at the Palace during royal visits to Malta in 1954, 1967 and 2005.

Queen Victoria's sixth child, Princess Louise, was one of the first members of the Royal Family to live at a Government House in Canada. The Princess arrived in 1878 with her husband, John, Marquess of Lorne (later 9th Duke of Argyll), when the Marquess took up the post of Governor-General of Canada. Their official residence was Rideau Hall in the new Canadian capital of Ottawa, although they travelled extensively through the Canadian prairies, visiting many of the Vice-Regal residences across the country during the five years that they spent in Canada.

In June 1883, Princess Louise welcomed her young nephew, Prince George of Wales (later King George V), to Rideau Hall when he arrived in Canada as a midshipman in the Royal Navy for his first tour of the dominion and he stayed with his aunt and uncle. Though it was not his first visit to a Government House.

Together with his older brother, Prince Albert Victor of Wales, the young Prince George of Wales had spent several years from 1879, serving on HMS *Bacchante*, accompanied by their tutor, John Neale Dalton. The brothers would tour many overseas territories of the British Empire as midshipmen in the Royal Navy and their travels would take them to the Caribbean, South Africa and Australia, stopping off at various Government Houses along the way. They also visited the United States, parts of South America, Egypt and the Far East, and had an

Sophie Lenoir/Shutterstock 627705251

Right: The palatial San Anton Palace, the official residence of the President of Malta, was previously a Government House of the British Empire and was the scene of the birth of the only royal child to be born at a Government House.

The Royal Family and Government Houses

audience with the Emperor of Japan, and were estimated to have travelled over 45,000 miles (72,000 kilometres). After his older brother went to Trinity College at Cambridge University, Prince George continued to serve with the Royal Navy and visit numerous nations abroad.

In 1901, Prince George, now titled the Duke of Cornwall and York following the death of Queen Victoria and his father's accession as King Edward VII, would undertake one of the biggest royal tours of the British Empire together with his wife, Princess Victoria Mary, Duchess of Cornwall and York (later Queen Mary). Originally said to have been planned for the Prince and Princess of Wales (later King Edward VII and Queen Alexandra), the sovereign's death on 22 January 1901 prevented them from undertaking the tour and so the Duke and Duchess of Cornwall and York took their places. The 1901 royal tour on HMS *Ophir* would include Gibraltar, Malta, Aden, Ceylon, Singapore, Australia, New Zealand, Mauritius, South Africa, Canada and the then Colony of Newfoundland (which had not yet joined the Confederation of Canada).

Coming so soon after the sovereign's death, the royal court was still in mourning and so the Duke and Duchess, as well as their private secretaries, equerries and ladies-in-waiting, spent much of the eight-month tour dressed in black. However, they frequently had the opportunity to stay at many Government Houses in the national capitals, states, provinces and territories that they visited and it was also an occasion for many of the Government Houses to take the opportunity to decorate and renovate their residences in preparation for their royal visitors. This was the first time that many of the people of the British Empire had the chance to see a future monarch and their consort up-close, and so their presence was widely celebrated wherever the royal couple went.

One of their most important duties during the royal tour was the opening of the first session of the new Parliament of the Commonwealth of Australia at the Exhibition Buildings in Melbourne on 9 May 1901, after the passing of the *Commonwealth of Australia Constitution Act 1900*. The royal couple stayed at Government House in Melbourne during this part of their visit and the Duke presented thousands of specially-designed war medals to colonial troops following the South African War.

History and Art Collection/Alamy PA86OG

Left: The Duke and Duchess of Cornwall and York (later King George V and Queen Mary) are pictured on the far right of this group photograph taken on the steps of Government House in Toronto, Canada during the 1901 royal tour. Many of the women, including the Duchess and her ladies-in-waiting, were dressed in black as the royal court was still officially in mourning for the late Queen Victoria.

Right: Prince Arthur, Duke of Connaught and Strathearn (front row, centre) pictured with his wife, Princess Louise Margaret, Duchess of Connaught (front row, fourth from the left) and their younger daughter, Princess Patricia of Connaught (front row, second from the left) during his term of office as the 10th Governor-General of Canada. The royal entourage are pictured dressed appropriately for the snowy Canadian winter.

Historic Collection/Alamy DRC88P

An interesting footnote to the 1901 royal tour is that the royal party included Prince Alexander of Teck, the youngest brother of the Duchess of Cornwall and York and later the Earl of Athlone, who would subsequently play an important part in the story of Government Houses as a future Governor-General of both South Africa and Canada.

The last of Queen Victoria's children to have a direct role in the history of Government Houses was Prince Arthur, Duke of Connaught and Strathearn, the Queen's third son. The 19-year-old Prince Arthur had been the first royal visitor to Canada following Confederation, when he arrived in 1869 for a military tour of Canada and the United States and stayed at Rideau Hall, the Vice-Regal residence of Canada. The then Governor-General, Sir Howard Elphinstone, said at the time that he hoped that the Prince might someday return as Governor-General, little knowing that his wish would be realised more than 40 years later in 1911. Prince Arthur had toured the British Empire in both his military and royal roles, representing King Edward VII at the Coronation Durbar in Delhi, India, in 1903 and representing King George V at the opening of the new Parliament of South Africa in 1910.

Prince Arthur was resident at Rideau Hall in Canada from 1911 to 1916 as the 10th Governor-General of Canada along with his wife, Princess Louise Margaret, Duchess of Connaught, and their younger daughter, Princess Patricia of Connaught, who often deputised for her mother at official functions. The artistic Princess Patricia had a painting studio at Rideau Hall, just as her aunt Princess Louise had before her, and she became a focal point for young women in Canada as they took an interest in the young Princess's activities and her favoured pastimes of ice skating and music.

In 1913, when the Duchess of Connaught began suffering from peritonitis while in Canada, and she returned to England for treatment, Princess Patricia began to officially stand in for her mother as the Vice-Regal Consort and accompanied her father on many public and official engagements at provincial Government Houses and elsewhere across Canada. In 1914, at the outbreak of the First World War, a military regiment was formed in Canada which became known as Princess Patricia's Canadian Light Infantry, with the Princess given the position as the regiment's first Colonel-in-Chief. It was to be a lifelong relationship between the regiment and Princess Patricia, who personally embroidered the first colour of the regiment that was carried into battle in the First World War and took an ongoing interest in the regiment's activities. The talented Princess was also said to have helped to design their military badge.

The Royal Family and Government Houses

History Collection/Alamy J4Cl6C

Princess Patricia would have fond memories of Rideau Hall in Canada for another reason as well. In October 1911, a young naval officer named Captain Alexander Ramsay had arrived from England to become the naval Aide-de-Camp to the Duke of Connaught in his role as Governor-General. Romance blossomed between the Princess and Captain Ramsay and in 1919, they would marry with the Princess relinquishing her royal titles to become Lady Patricia Ramsay.

Left: Princess Patricia of Connaught presents regimental colours to the Canadian regiment, Princess Patricia's Canadian Light Infantry, as their first Colonel-in-Chief. It was a relationship that began when she spent time with her parents at Government House in Canada.

The Connaught family would continue to have a role in the history of Government Houses for successive generations. Between 1920 and 1924, Princess Patricia's brother, Prince Arthur of Connaught, named after his father, would serve as Governor-General of South Africa and occupy the Vice-Regal Government Houses of South Africa in Cape Town, Pretoria and Johannesburg. He was accompanied to South Africa as Vice-Regal Consort by his wife, Princess Arthur of Connaught, Duchess of Fife in her own right and a great-granddaughter of Queen Victoria.

Sadly their son, Prince Alastair, 2nd Duke of Connaught, would unfortunately meet a tragic end at Rideau Hall in Canada, aged just 28. The young army officer was posted to Canada to serve as Aide-de-Camp to the Governor-General when he died in 1943 as a result of hypothermia, said to have been the result of falling down inebriated by an open window in the middle of winter. A brass plaque commemorates his life in St Bartholomew's Church opposite Rideau Hall and another memorial can be found in Scotland at St Ninian's Chapel, Braemar, the chapel of the Dukes of Fife on the Mar Lodge Estate.

The Governor-General in Canada at the time of the Prince's tragic death was the Earl of Athlone, the aforementioned Prince Alexander of Teck. The younger brother of Queen Mary, Prince Alexander had been proposed as a successor to Prince Arthur, Duke of Connaught, as Governor-General of Canada in 1914, however a Member of the Canadian Parliament had objected to someone with a German princely title taking the role of Governor-General during the First World War. This criticism turned out to be somewhat ironic, as Prince Alexander had signed up to serve in the war with the British Army. In 1917, when King George V removed the Germanic titles used in the British Royal Family, Prince Alexander of Teck would become the Earl of Athlone with the surname of Cambridge, although his wife, Princess Alice, Countess of Athlone, would retain her royal rank as she had been born a British Princess and a granddaughter of Queen Victoria.

The Earl of Athlone would serve as Governor-General of South Africa from 1924 to 1931 and then as Governor-General of Canada from 1940 to 1946, during a critical time in the history of both countries in the 20th century. The Athlones would take up residence and visit many Government Houses of the Commonwealth as a result of these overseas roles.

Their time in South Africa was turbulent, as the country struggled with the racial and political tensions of the 1920s. The Athlones arrived early in 1924 to open the South Africa Union Parliament and they worked quietly behind the scenes to try to bring together all sections of society. Princess Alice took a great interest in South African charities and was

Above: As Governor-General of Canada, the Earl of Athlone, hosted the 1943 and 1944 Québec Conferences to discuss wartime strategies at his official residence, La Citadelle. This photograph from 1944 shows the royal couple and their guests facing the world's media, overlooking the St Lawrence River. From left to right: Mrs Clementine Churchill; the Earl of Athlone; President Franklin D. Roosevelt of the United States of America; Princess Alice, Countess of Athlone; Mr Winston Churchill, Prime Minister of Great Britain; Mrs Eleanor Roosevelt; and Canadian Prime Minister, William L. Mackenzie King.

particularly fond of one of their official residences at Government House in Cape Town. Known as 'De Tuynhuys' (or The Garden House), the residence is known for its formal and informal gardens in a beautiful setting within sight of Table Mountain. It is an official residence for the President of South Africa today.

In 1928, the death of their son, Viscount Trematon, in a car accident in France was a particular blow to the royal couple, however the outpouring of sympathy from all over South Africa in particular, as well as the Commonwealth, demonstrated the affection in which Princess Alice and the Earl of Athlone were held. It was with much sadness that the Athlones left South Africa in 1931.

In 1940, King George VI received a telegram from the Canadian Prime Minister, William L. Mackenzie King, suggesting the King's uncle, the Earl of Athlone, as the next Governor-General of Canada. The Earl was extremely flattered to be asked, but he thought that a younger man should be appointed. He was persuaded by his nephew to take up the position for an initial two years.

In the end, the Athlones stayed for five years, during one of the most important periods of global history when Canada was engaged in the Second World War. They welcomed President Franklin D. Roosevelt of the United States of America, Prime Minister Winston Churchill of Great Britain and Mackenzie King to their residence, La Citadelle in Québec for the 1943 and 1944 Québec Conferences to discuss wartime strategies.

During their time in Canada as the Vice-Regal couple, when their official residence was Rideau Hall in Ottawa, it became home to numerous displaced and exiled royals from Europe due to the Second World War, many of them related to Princess Alice. One of King George VI's nephews, George Lascelles, later Earl of Harewood, would serve as the Aide-de-Camp to the Governor-General of Canada at Rideau Hall in 1945–46, a position that his father had held as Viscount Lascelles in 1904–06.

The Royal Family and Government Houses

Princess Alice, Countess of Athlone, would continue to visit Government Houses in many different parts of the Commonwealth, particularly after the death of the Earl of Athlone in 1957. In Queensland, Australia, Princess Alice visited her daughter, Lady May Abel Smith and her son-in-law, Sir Henry Abel Smith several times when they were residents of Government House in Brisbane during Sir Henry's tenure as the Governor of Queensland from 1958 to 1966.

Princess Alice also stayed in several Government Houses in the Caribbean when she was Chancellor of the University of the West Indies and the Princess would combine her annual duties at the university with a winter holiday each year. She also returned to South Africa a number of times to visit her many friends and would revisit the former Vice-Regal residences that were her homes in the 1920s.

In Australia, Government House in Canberra and its counterpart Admiralty House in Sydney underwent redecoration in the early 1940s in anticipation of the expected appointment of the younger brother of King George VI, Prince George, Duke of Kent, and his glamorous wife, Princess Marina, as the next Governor-General of Australia and the Vice-Regal Consort. Sadly, the combination of the onset of the Second World War and the subsequent sudden death of Prince George in an aeroplane crash in 1942 meant that this plan was never realised. However, Prince George's elder brother, Prince Henry, Duke of Gloucester, accepted the appointment in 1945, becoming the first and only member of the Royal Family to be the Governor-General of Australia.

It was not Prince Henry's first visit to a Government House of the Commonwealth as he had undertaken a far-reaching official tour of nearly three months to Australia and New Zealand in 1934–35 when he stayed at Vice-Regal residences in both countries. However, when he arrived as Governor-General in 1945, he was accompanied on that occasion by his wife Princess Alice, Duchess of Gloucester, and their two young sons, Princes William and Richard of Gloucester, who would live at Government House in Canberra for two years.

Left: When Prince Henry, Duke of Gloucester became the first and only member of the Royal Family to be the Governor-General of Australia between 1945 and 1947, he would take up residence at Government House in Canberra. This postage stamp from the period commemorates the appointment.

Right: The Duke of Windsor, and his wife, the Duchess of Windsor, who lived at Government House in Nassau when the Duke was appointed as Governor of The Bahamas in 1940, take part in one of their many Vice-Regal duties during their time in The Bahamas.

Chronicle/Alamy DRHHB4

Princess Alice would find that the residence posed a number of challenges, particularly with the ever-changing extremes of weather and the snakes and spiders that found their way into the building, but the young Princes certainly enjoyed the vast gardens.

Another royal resident of a Government House around this time was the Duke of Windsor (previously King Edward VIII) and his wife, the Duchess of Windsor (the former Wallis Simpson). The Duke was appointed as the Governor of The Bahamas from 1940 to 1945, during the Second World War, and they lived at Government House in Nassau. The appointment was seen as strategic, as it placed the Duke and Duchess away from the wartime dangers of living in France where they had originally settled, while not bringing them back to Britain where they may cause embarrassment to the Royal Family.

The Duke of Windsor was no stranger to Government Houses as he had travelled to the far reaches of the British Empire as a youthful Prince of Wales in the early part of the 20th century, with vast tours of Canada, India, Australia and New Zealand amongst others. He was also a regular visitor to Alberta in Canada over many years, where he had acquired a rural ranch as a private residence.

At the beginning of 1947, Lord Louis Mountbatten was appointed as the first and only royal Viceroy of India and Governor-General of India. The two titles had been combined since 1858 and the position was one of the most important in the post-war period, when India was moving towards independence. Lord Mountbatten was a distant cousin of King George VI, but he was very close to the Royal Family and his nephew, Prince Philip of Greece, was about to marry Princess Elizabeth. Recently created Viscount Mountbatten of Burma (later Earl Mountbatten of Burma), he had a distinguished military record, particularly in the Far East during the Second World War. Lord Mountbatten arrived in India to take up residence with his wife, Lady Edwina, and their younger daughter, Lady Pamela, in the huge Government House, often known as the Viceroy's House.

The Royal Family and Government Houses

The newly built Government House in Delhi had been inaugurated in 1931 to replace previous Government Houses in India after the capital moved to Delhi and it was designed by Sir Edwin Lutyens on a grand scale. The Mountbattens would only stay for little over a year, and today, the residence is known as *Rashtrapati Bhavan* and is the official residence of the President of India.

Throughout the British administration of India, the Governors-General also had the use of the Vice-Regal Lodge, known as *Rashtrapati Niwas*, in the mountains at Shimla, where they would escape the heat of the summer. The government of India would also move with them. The post of Viceroy was abolished in August 1947 when India gained independence and Lord Mountbatten would remain for another ten months as the Governor-General of India, a position that continued until India became a republic in 1950.

King George VI and Queen Elizabeth stayed at many Government Houses when they undertook a royal tour to Australia and New Zealand in 1927 (as the Duke and Duchess of York), where they opened the new Parliament of Australia in Canberra, and also in 1939 during their royal tour of Canada and the United States.

Queen Elizabeth II first visited several Government Houses when she was Princess Elizabeth during the 1947 three-month visit to South Africa, Southern Rhodesia (now Zimbabwe) and Bechuanaland (now Botswana) with her parents, King George VI and Queen Elizabeth, and her younger sister, Princess Margaret.

Although the Royal Family toured the country on the famous ivory-painted White Train, with its air-conditioned saloons and sleeping compartments, they also visited several Government Houses during the royal tour, in particular Government House in Cape Town where the Connaughts and the Athlones had had their official residence in the 1920s. It was while visiting Government House in Cape Town that Princess Elizabeth celebrated her 21st birthday with a special ball.

Left: In 1947, King George VI is photographed presenting an award during the royal visit to Bechuanaland (now Botswana) watched by Queen Elizabeth, Princess Elizabeth and Princess Margaret. Accompanying the Royal Family in the role of the King's Equerry was Group Captain Peter Townsend (front right) who would later become romantically involved with Princess Margaret.

Right: A commemorative souvenir of the Coronation tour of 1953–54. The royal tour would be one of the most ambitious in history and it would take Queen Elizabeth II and Prince Philip to Government Houses all over the Commonwealth.

On their return journey to England from South Africa on-board HMS *Vanguard*, King George VI paid the first visit by a reigning monarch to the island of St Helena in the Atlantic Ocean, accompanied by Queen Elizabeth and the Princesses Elizabeth and Margaret. There was doubt that the Princesses would visit the island, as they were said to be suffering from heavy colds and were expected to stay on the ship, but they accompanied their parents at the last minute. After a carriage tour of the island and a visit to Napoleon's former residence at Longwood House, the royal party visited Plantation House, St Helena's Government House, for tea and they met the famous tortoises in its grounds.

Following their marriage in 1947, Princess Elizabeth, Duchess of Edinburgh, and the Duke of Edinburgh visited Canada in 1951 for a two-month royal tour that extended from the Maritime Provinces on the Atlantic Ocean (Newfoundland, Prince Edward Island and Nova Scotia) across Central Canada (Québec and Ontario) to the Prairie Provinces (Manitoba, Saskatchewan and Alberta) and West Coast (British Columbia) on the Pacific Ocean. They stayed in many Government Houses all over Canada and attended receptions, dinners, investitures, garden parties and numerous other official functions at the Vice-Regal residences where they were based. During this visit, the royal couple also visited Washington, DC to stay at the White House for two days with President Harry S. Truman of the United States of America.

A planned visit to Australia and New Zealand by King George VI and Queen Elizabeth in 1949 had been cancelled due to the King's ill health, but on 31 January 1952, Princess Elizabeth and the Duke of Edinburgh set off on a royal tour of Australia and New Zealand, with a stop-over in Kenya on route. On their arrival in Nairobi, they were entertained by the Governor of Kenya, Sir Philip Mitchell, and attended a garden party at Government House, Nairobi, before a civic lunch and a trip to a national park the following day. Today, the former Government House in Nairobi is State House, the official residence of the President of Kenya, and it was visited in 2018 by The Queen's grandson, Prince William, who was received there by President Uhuru Kenyatta.

The royal couple moved onto the Sagana Lodge, a wedding gift from Kenya, where they were to stay for a few days before their departure for Australia. However, the royal tour was postponed once again when the King died on 6 February 1952 and the young Princess became Queen Elizabeth II.

Within five months of her coronation in 1953, Queen Elizabeth II and Prince Philip set out on the Royal Family's most ambitious overseas trip, featuring many royal firsts, and one that would take them to Government Houses all over the Commonwealth. It would be the longest royal tour, covering over 44,000 miles (70,000 kilometres) and it was said to include 12 tons (12,000 kgs) of luggage. The royal couple took a plane to Bermuda to stay for a few days at Government House near Hamilton, and went onto Jamaica for their first visit

The Royal Family and Government Houses

by a reigning monarch. They then boarded the SS *Gothic*, a huge ship that would take the royal party to Fiji and Tonga, where the young Queen Elizabeth II would be reunited with Queen Sālote of Tonga who had attended her coronation in London earlier in the year. The journey continued to New Zealand where the royal couple spent Christmas at Government House in Auckland and toured the country for over a month. It was during this stay that The Queen broadcast her Christmas radio message to the Commonwealth for that year from Government House in Auckland, as well as hosting a garden party and children's party in the grounds. It was the first time that New Zealand had welcomed their monarch and The Queen was enthusiastically received all over the country.

In February 1954, Queen Elizabeth II became the first reigning monarch to set foot on Australian soil at Farm Cove in Sydney, before embarking on a visit that took in most of the state capitals and covered many thousands of miles. Australia had never seen anything like the royal tour before and the royal couple stayed in Government Houses across the country. The return journey of the Coronation tour included Ceylon, Uganda, Aden and Malta, where The Queen and the Duke of Edinburgh were reunited with their two children, Prince Charles and Princess Anne, and together they sailed via Gibraltar to London on the new Royal Yacht *Britannia*.

This was the first of many such tours during The Queen's reign and as air travel became more widespread, the monarch and the Royal Family were able to go to almost every part of the Commonwealth and they would stay at many Government Houses during their visits. There followed a period of transition as the British Empire evolved into the modern Commonwealth that we see today, with many nations becoming independent, either as Commonwealth realms with Queen Elizabeth II as their head of state or as republics with a directly elected President, but remaining a member of the Commonwealth. Many members of the Royal Family represented The Queen at the ceremonies of independence that took place between the 1950s and the 1980s, although all retained close links to the monarchy.

Many Government Houses across the Commonwealth also began to adapt and change to the new circumstances, while still retaining their unique status at the centre of official life. However, both current and former Government Houses remained ready to welcome the sovereign and members of the Royal Family on their official visits.

In the 1970s, The Queen undertook 73 overseas trips and visited 48 different countries. In 1977, during The Queen's Silver Jubilee year, celebrations took place across the United Kingdom and the Commonwealth. The Queen and Prince Philip toured the UK and official overseas visits were also made to Western Samoa, Australia, New Zealand, Tonga, Fiji, Tasmania, Papua New Guinea, Canada and the West Indies. It was estimated that the royal couple travelled 56,000 miles (90,000 kilometres) during that year.

Royal children had traditionally not accompanied their parents on royal tours overseas. In 1954, towards the end of the Coronation tour, the Queen's young children, Prince Charles and Princess Anne, travelled out to Malta to stay with their great-uncle and great-aunt, Lord Louis and Lady Edwina Mountbatten, as he was stationed there at the time. The royal children were able to meet their parents and travel with them back to the United Kingdom on-board the Royal Yacht *Britannia*.

The first royal baby to be allowed to travel on a royal tour was Prince William in 1983 when he went to Australia and New Zealand with his parents, the Prince and Princess of Wales. The one-year-old Prince was famously photographed with his parents by the media during an official photo-call in the gardens of Government House in Auckland, New Zealand.

The practice was repeated over 30 years later, when 18-month-old Prince George of Cambridge travelled to Australia and New Zealand in 2014 with his parents, the Duke and Duchess of Cambridge, and stayed at Admiralty House in Sydney and Government House in Wellington. In 2016, Prince George was off on his travels again, this time with his sister,

Right: The Prince of Wales and the Duchess of Cornwall are welcomed to a reception held at Government House in Sydney by Hon. David Hurley, the Governor of New South Wales and Mrs Linda Hurley during the royal couple's tour of Australia in November 2015.

Princess Charlotte, when they travelled to British Columbia in Canada with their parents. A special children's tea party was held for military families as well as the royal children in the grounds of Government House, British Columbia where they were staying during the royal tour.

In 2002, another busy programme of visits both within the United Kingdom and overseas took place to mark The Queen's Golden Jubilee and 50 years of her reign. The Queen and Prince Philip went to Jamaica, New Zealand, Australia and Canada, visiting many Government Houses on their way, as well as going to every region of the United Kingdom. The Queen's Diamond Jubilee in 2012 saw The Queen and the Duke of Edinburgh travel as widely as possible across England, Scotland, Wales and Northern Ireland, touring every region.

Due to the royal couple's advancing years, the Royal Family represented the monarch on trips to many of the Commonwealth realms, British Overseas Territories and other Commonwealth countries to mark the Diamond Jubilee. The Diamond Jubilee royal tours included many visits to current and former Government Houses by members of the Royal Family in one of the most extensive joint royal tours in recent times.

The Prince of Wales and the Duchess of Cornwall went to Australia, Canada, New Zealand and Papua New Guinea. The Prince of Wales also visited the Crown Dependencies of the Channel Islands, Jersey and Guernsey, and the Isle of Man. The Duke and Duchess of Cambridge travelled to Malaysia, Singapore, the Solomon Islands and Tuvalu while Prince Harry undertook Diamond Jubilee visits to Belize, Jamaica and The Bahamas. The Duke of York went to India, while the Earl and Countess of Wessex toured the Caribbean (Antigua and Barbuda, Barbados, Grenada, Montserrat, St Kitts and Nevis, St Lucia, St Vincent and the Grenadines, Trinidad and Tobago) and also visited Gibraltar. The Princess Royal went to Mozambique and Zambia, while the Duke of Gloucester travelled to the Virgin Islands and Malta, and the Duke of Kent visited the Falkland Islands and Uganda.

Queen Elizabeth II and Prince Philip are the most travelled members of the Royal Family in history with The Queen estimated to have covered more than a million miles (1.6 million kilometres), equivalent to journeying around the world over 40 times. The Queen has undertaken official visits to more than 120 countries - including the Commonwealth realms such as Canada, Australia and New Zealand; British Overseas Territories and Crown Dependencies; many Commonwealth countries especially in Africa, the Caribbean, Asia and the Pacific; almost every country in Europe, including France, Germany, Spain and Italy; numerous independent countries across the world, such as Libya, Iran, Nepal, Thailand, Brazil, Chile, Mexico, Russia and the United States. The last overseas visit made by The Queen was to Malta in November 2015.

Queen Elizabeth II and the Royal Family have followed in the footsteps of previous royal generations in travelling the world. During these overseas visits and tours, the many Government Houses across the Commonwealth have played host to members of the Royal Family and provided a vital link between the Crown and the people.

The Royal Family and Government Houses

Commonwealth Realms

A Commonwealth realm is a sovereign state or country that has a constitutional monarch as their head of state that is shared with others, but retains a crown legally distinct from the other realms.

The 1931 Statute of Westminster in the Parliament of the United Kingdom provided for the then Dominions – at the time, Canada, Australia, New Zealand, the Union of South Africa, the Irish Free State and Newfoundland to have independence as equal members of the British Commonwealth of Nations and share the same person as their sovereign.

By the early 1950s, in order to reflect the equality between the countries in this group, each became known as a realm. The term was formally used in the proclamation of Elizabeth II as Queen in 1952. The monarch is represented by a Governor-General in all realms except for the United Kingdom, and the Governor-General is appointed by the sovereign on the advice of the Ministers of the country concerned (except in Papua New Guinea, where the Governor-General is elected by the Legislature) and is completely independent of the British Government. The Governors-General usually reside in Government House.

The sovereign maintains direct contact with the Governors-General, although Executive power is delegated to them in virtually every respect. In some of the larger Commonwealth realms that operate a federal system, for example in Australia and Canada, the sovereign is represented by a Governor or Lieutenant-Governor at a state level and by the Governor-General at the national level.

The current Commonwealth realms are: Antigua and Barbuda; Australia; The Bahamas; Barbados; Belize; Canada; Grenada; Jamaica; New Zealand; Papua New Guinea; St Kitts and Nevis; St Lucia; St Vincent and the Grenadines; Solomon Islands; Tuvalu; and the United Kingdom.

Alex Cimbal/Shutterstock 1146815858

Government House, Antigua and Barbuda

Antigua and Barbuda lies in the north-east Caribbean in the middle of the Leeward Islands and has a population of about 80,000 people across its two main islands. The country's name was reputed to have been given by the explorer Christopher Columbus in 1493, in honour of the Virgin of La Antigua in Seville Cathedral, Spain.

The English settled on Antigua in 1632, with the smaller island of Barbuda being settled in 1684. Antigua and Barbuda became independent in 1981 as a Commonwealth realm, although it retains strong links to the United Kingdom. The head of state is Queen Elizabeth II and the monarch is represented by the Governor-General of Antigua and Barbuda. The capital and largest port is St John's on Antigua, which is also the location of Government House, the official residence and office of the Governor-General.

For the first 150 years of there being Governors and Administrators of Antigua and Barbuda, there was no official Vice-Regal residence and most incumbents either already had a property on the islands or rented a suitable home. In the 1800s, as St John's became the main trading and business town in Antigua, it was decided that a fitting residence should be acquired for the Governors of Antigua and Barbuda.

A large house called the 'Parsonage', which had been built in the 1700s in the Georgian style, was selected as Government House and upgraded significantly, including the diversion of one of the nearby roads to allow further expansion of the property. The first Governor to live at Government House was Sir Ralph Payne, Lord Lavington.

Further major additions to the building took place in 1860 in preparation for the royal visit of Prince Alfred, Duke of Edinburgh, during a naval tour of the Caribbean. The oldest parts of the house are the dining room and living room that are still used today for official functions, although much of the property is in need of restoration. Many

All images: The 18th century Government House in St John's has seen many royal visitors over the years. The historic residence is under constant scrutiny to protect its architectural features.

interesting items and historical artefacts can be found within including furniture, china and paintings with royal insignia.

Government House in Antigua and Barbuda has welcomed numerous royal visitors over the years, including Queen Elizabeth II and Prince Philip in 1966 during their Caribbean tour and again in 1977 for their Silver Jubilee tour. Princess Margaret was particularly fond of the islands, first visiting in 1955 during a royal tour of the Caribbean and returning for her honeymoon in 1960. She became the Patron of the fundraising project for the restoration of another historic residence on Antigua. This property was originally the Commissioner's House where King William IV, also Duke of Clarence, was said to have lived as a young naval officer in the 1780s, when he was serving in the Royal Navy with Admiral Nelson. The building was named 'Clarence House' after him, as was his London residence of the same name. Although Princess Margaret did not live to see the restoration project completed, her great-nephew, Prince Henry of Wales, was present for the opening of the renovated Clarence House in November 2016, during a visit to Antigua and Barbuda on the occasion of the 35th anniversary of its independence.

The Prince of Wales also visited Antigua and Barbuda in November 2017 to see the relief effort following the devastation caused by Hurricane Irma earlier in September of the same year, which left up to 95% of Barbuda's houses and commercial buildings destroyed.

Antigua and Barbuda

Government House, Canberra

Australia became a Commonwealth realm in 1901, when the *Constitution of Australia* was adopted and the country became independent of Great Britain. The sovereign became the King or Queen of Australia and since then has been represented by a Governor-General. Australia is the world's sixth largest country by area and is made up of the mainland plus the island of Tasmania and several smaller islands. Australia was inhabited by indigenous peoples for around 60,000 years before the first British settlements in the late 18th century, although it was the Dutch who claimed to have been the first Europeans to settle there.

The British First Fleet, under the command of Captain Arthur Phillip, raised the flag at Sydney Cove in New South Wales on 26 January 1788, a date that would become recognised as 'Australia Day'. The first European settlers founded several penal colonies in the east of the country and the population grew as more settlements and trading were established. In the 19th century, several states and territories were formed and, on 1 January 1901, the states federated to create the Commonwealth of Australia. Today, the population is around 25 million people, which is heavily concentrated on the eastern and south-eastern coastlines.

The Governor-General of Australia is the head of the Executive branch of the federal government, serving as the Vice-Regal representative of the Australian monarch. The Governor-General's position has no fixed term, but usually serves for around five years. The official residence of the Governor-General of Australia is Government House in Canberra, the country's capital city. The residence is often known as Yarralumla, named after the suburb in which it is located and where many overseas embassies are also found. Unlike most state Government Houses in the Australian states and territories which were built during Queen Victoria's reign as homes for Vice-Regal representatives, Yarralumla didn't become a Vice-Regal residence until the 20th century.

Between 1901 and 1927, when the Commonwealth of Australia was first established, the Governor-General resided in Government House in Melbourne, which was the federal capital of the new country and the seat of both the national parliament and government. In 1913, the area that later became the city of Canberra was chosen to be the site of the new federal capital city of Australia, located almost midway between its two rival cities, Melbourne and Sydney. The Australian federal government acquired a large 'station' or farm at Yarralumla dating from the 1830s, which became the site of the Vice-Regal residence.

Due to the First World War and the post-war economic conditions that followed, the Australian federal government didn't move to the new capital in Canberra until 1927 and the Governor-General of Australia continued to live primarily at Government House in Melbourne until 1930, when that building was returned to the Governor of Victoria.

The first stone lodge on the site at Yarralumla was built in the 1830s for Francis Mowatt and the property changed hands many times before it came into the Campbell family. A large Georgian-style house, the core part of the existing Government House in Canberra dates from around 1890–91 and was built by farmer Frederick Campbell as a three-storey, red-brick house at the centre of a working sheep station. In the years after the property was purchased by the federal government in 1913, major renovations were undertaken, and a three-storey extension and a new entrance were built. The basic structure of the 1891 house can still clearly be seen and the Campbell family crest can be found on the exterior of the building, but very little remains of the old stone lodge.

The first Governor-General of Australia to stay at Government House in Canberra was Lord Stonehaven. He welcomed the first royal visitors to Yarralumla when Prince Albert, Duke of York, and his wife, Elizabeth, Duchess of York (later King George VI and Queen Elizabeth), came to Canberra to open the new Australian Parliament (now Old Parliament House) in 1927 on behalf of King George V.

Martin Darley/Shutterstock 53483674

Above: The extensive grounds of Government House of around 133 acres (54 hectares) gives the estate in Canberra a tranquil feel.

Government House in Canberra was never meant to be the permanent official residence of the Governor-General as it was considered small in comparison to other Australian Government Houses. Yet the economic depression of the 1920s and 1930s, followed by the Second World War, meant that plans for a new Government House never materialised.

Prior to the royal visit in 1927, Government House in Canberra had further remodelling work and interior decorations undertaken by the then Commonwealth Architect, John Smith Murdoch, and interiors and furniture designed by Ruth Lane Poole of the Australian Federal Capital Commission. Formal reception rooms for royal and Vice-Regal functions led on to more informal private apartments for the Governor-General and official guest suites, which remain today.

In 1939, yet more extensive renovations were undertaken and a new 'state entrance' was built on the northern side of the house. Further bedrooms and a nursery were added, and the drawing room was extended. A new private sitting room over the south entrance porch was constructed at around this time, with a wide window framing the 'vista' or views of the gardens and beyond to the Brindabella Ranges and the foothills of the Australian Alps in the distance. This became a suite of rooms known as the 'Vista Suite' which is often where the monarch or senior guests stay.

The changes to the house at this time were precipitated by the expected appointment of the younger son of King George V, Prince George, Duke of Kent, and his glamorous wife, Princess Marina, Duchess of Kent, as the next Governor-General of Australia and Vice-Regal Consort. Sadly, Prince George was killed in an airplane crash in 1942 during the Second World War and his elder brother, Prince Henry, Duke of Gloucester, was later appointed to the role in 1945.

All of the changes to Government House were completed for the arrival of the first and only royal Governor-General of Australia, the Duke of Gloucester, who lived at the residence with his wife, Princess Alice, Duchess of Gloucester, and their two young sons, Princes William and Richard of Gloucester, between 1945 and 1947. Princess Alice later wrote in her memoirs that living at Government House gave the family many challenges due to the dramatic changes in weather in Canberra, from searing heat to glacial cold in a very short space of time. However, despite some of the difficulties of the residence and the weather compared to back home in England, the Duchess remembered her young sons enjoying the wide open spaces of the vast gardens, and the generous and welcoming staff.

Australia

The centre of Government House has a wood-panelled State Entrance Hall lined with Australian art including a study portrait by Sir William Dargie for the famous 'wattle portrait' of Queen Elizabeth II as Queen of Australia. The State Dining Room is located on the lakefront side of the house, and features a large bay window and terrace overlooking Lake Burley Griffin.

The furnishings, artworks and decorations in Government House reflect a wide range of different Australian artists and craftspeople, including a large collection of artworks by indigenous artists. Many Australian institutions, including the National Gallery of Australia, the National Library of Australia and The Australiana Fund, have lent much of the furniture and art objects in the house.

Today at Government House, the Governor-General holds meetings of the Australian Federal Executive Council, receives the Prime Minister, other government officials and foreign ambassadors, and holds investitures for the Order of Australia. The residence is the setting for state dinners for visiting royalty and heads of state, as well as functions for community and special needs groups. On visits to Australia, Queen Elizabeth II, as head of state, and members of the Royal Family stay at Government House in Canberra. The Queen has been to Australia many times, the first in 1954 when she became the first reigning monarch to be welcomed there, followed by 15 further visits until 2012. Many members of the Royal Family have toured Australia in the intervening years and most royal visitors will enjoy the hospitality at Government House in the national capital city.

Government House is set in 133 acres (54 hectares) of extensive parkland and landscaped gardens which surround the house. The gardens were first created by horticulturalist Charles Weston, and many of the trees in the gardens have been planted by royal and distinguished visitors. The 'English garden' was planted by Lady Gowrie, wife of the Governor-General in the early 1940s, and it includes a memorial to their only surviving son, Patrick Hore-Ruthven, who was killed in the Second World War.

A garden of bravery has also been established in the grounds, which contains a number of memorials to Australian civilian and military heroes including holders of the Victoria Cross, and the memorial garden was added to in 2000 when granite pillars were installed to represent the stars of the Southern Cross constellation.

Above: The rear of Government House in Canberra has a terrace with views over Lake Burley Griffin.

Jeffrey Hyland

Admiralty House, Sydney

Few would disagree that Sydney has one of the most beautiful natural harbours in the world. It is fitting, therefore, that when royal and distinguished guests visit this vibrant Australian city, they often stay at one of its oldest and most exclusive addresses overlooking the harbour.

Admiralty House is the official Sydney residence of the Governor-General of Australia and as such it is placed at the disposal of Queen Elizabeth II and the Royal Family when they are visiting Sydney in an official capacity, as well as hosting world leaders, Presidents and even the Pope. An elegant colonial-style house in the discreet north Sydney suburb of Kirribilli, Admiralty House occupies a beautiful harbour-side location, with fine views of the world-famous Sydney Opera House and the Harbour Bridge.

The oldest part of the existing house was built in 1845–46 by Lieutenant Colonel John Gibbes, who was the Colonial Collector of Customs at a time when Australia was still an overseas territory of the vast British Empire. The single-storey, stone-built house was known by the local name of 'Wotonga', and had a wide verandah, and living quarters for a succession of early settlers' and merchants' families. In 1854, a side plot of land belonging to Admiralty House was sold and the property built there was later named Kirribilli House. Today, it is an official residence for the Australian Prime Minister on visits to Sydney.

Over the next 40 years, Sydney grew into an important naval port, becoming home to the Royal Navy's Australian Squadron under the command of a British Admiral of the Fleet. In 1885, Wotonga House was purchased by the New South Wales government, in the name of the Crown, as the official residence for the new naval Commander-in-Chief. The house was enlarged extensively, with the construction of a second storey along with the covered verandah that still exists today.

Above: Admiralty House is one of the oldest harbour-side properties in Sydney, Australia dating from 1845–46.

A large billiard room was also added to the house, as it was an essential requirement for any 'gentleman' of society in Victorian times. In late 1885, Vice-Admiral Sir George Tryon arrived to take command of the Australian Naval Squadron and to occupy the newly named Admiral's House, later to become Admiralty House. The naval commanders who occupied the property over the next 25 years are commemorated in the stained-glass windows on the

Australia

main staircase. Each coloured window bears the coat of arms of the 11 British Admirals who lived there from 1885–1913.

Two of the earliest royal visitors to Admiralty House were the Duke and Duchess of Cornwall and York (later King George V and Queen Mary) in 1901. The Duke and Duchess attended several engagements and receptions in Sydney during their stay including a naval reception at Admiralty House. Other distinguished visitors in the early 20th century included the explorers, Ernest Shackleton and Robert Falcon Scott, both on their epic voyages to the South Pole.

With the establishment of the Royal Australian Navy in 1909, the command of the Southern fleet was handed over to the Australian federal government and so there was no longer any requirement for a British Admiral to reside in Sydney. In October 1913, the 11th and final British Commander, Vice-Admiral Sir George King-Hall, lowered his flag at Admiralty House for the last time. The federal government had decided that Admiralty House should be used as the Sydney residence of the monarch's representative in Australia and, as such, Lord Denman was the first Governor-General of Australia to occupy the house in 1913.

Nearly 14 years later, Admiralty House once again played host to a royal visit by another Duke and Duchess of York – this time, the titles were held by Prince Albert and his wife, Elizabeth (later King George VI and Queen Elizabeth), who arrived in Sydney on HMS *Renown* to great acclaim from the estimated one million people lining the harbour on 26 March 1927. The Governor-General of Australia, Lord Stonehaven, entertained the Duke and Duchess of York at Admiralty House before they departed for Canberra to open the newly built federal Parliament.

Sadly, the effects of the economic depression of the late 1920s resulted in the closure of Admiralty House, which led to the auction of its contents in 1930. The house remained

empty and fell into disrepair until 1936 when the federal government decided to reopen it for the incoming Governor-General, Lord Gowrie. It has remained the Sydney home of the Governor-General ever since. The formal transfer of Admiralty House to the Commonwealth of Australia was made by Crown grant in 1948, on condition that it should only be used as an official residence for the Governor-General of Australia.

The first royal occupants of Admiralty House were Prince Henry, Duke of Gloucester, and his wife, Princess Alice, Duchess of Gloucester, who used the property regularly on their official visits to Sydney between 1945 and 1947, when the Duke was Governor-General of Australia.

It was another seven years before Queen Elizabeth II came to Admiralty House. The Queen arrived in Sydney on

Howard Mitchell

3 February 1954 as the first-ever reigning monarch to go to Australia. It was the first of many visits to Admiralty House over the years while undertaking engagements in Sydney, including notable occasions such as the opening of the Sydney Opera House in 1973 and the sesquicentenary of the founding of the city in 1992. Other members of the Royal Family have also stayed in the first-floor principal suite at Admiralty House in recent years, and receptions are often held there for visiting royalty and official guests.

Today, Admiralty House has been restored to the style of its late Victorian origins, with a series of tastefully decorated reception rooms that are furnished with early colonial furniture, porcelain, ornaments and many historical artworks, including portraits of explorer Captain James Cook and various former Governors-General of Australia. Many of the portraits and furniture are on loan from the Australian National Gallery and The Australiana Fund. The residence also features a large state dining room and the Governor-General's official study. It is here that the Governor-General can receive a wide range of charity and government delegations often connected with Sydney and New South Wales.

The ground floor of the house contains a vestibule and hallway, two reception rooms, a dining room, a study and an elaborate central staircase. The private bedroom suites are on the upper floors and have fine views across the harbour.

Throughout its history, Admiralty House has played host to British Admirals, Governors-General and several generations of the Royal Family and it continues to be a working residence for the monarch's representative in Australia today.

Jeffrey Hyland

Right: The main entrance to Admiralty House is located at the rear of the property.

Australia

Government House, New South Wales

As the location of the first European settlers to arrive in the country, the city of Sydney and the state of New South Wales, have played an important role in the national life and the development of Australia on the eastern coast. The Australian Crown is represented in each state by a Vice-Regal representative, usually a Governor, who undertakes ceremonial duties on behalf of the monarch at a state level in the same way that the Governor-General does at a national level. State Governors are appointed by the monarch on the advice of the Premier of the relevant state, usually for a period of five years.

Previous Government Houses

The first Government House in Sydney was constructed in 1788, although the building itself no longer survives. The property, along with Old Government House in the Sydney suburb of Parramatta, were the official residences of the first Governors of New South Wales for around 50 years.

The original Government House was built for the first Governor of the then Colony of New South Wales, Governor Arthur Phillip, who laid the foundation stone in Sydney's Bridge Street (today, the site of the Museum of Sydney). As one of the first permanent buildings in the newly established city, the first Government House had two storeys, built of English bricks and local sandstone, and featured six rooms and the first staircase in the country. At a later date, a verandah was added, said to be one of the first of its type in Australia. At the front was a small garden, where many imported plant species from England were grown. The house was developed under the supervision of James Bloodsworth, a convict builder responsible for the construction of many of Sydney's early buildings between 1788 and 1800.

The house was at the heart of the political and cultural life of New South Wales, but the lifespan of the property was short-lived due to the quality of the building materials, and submissions were made to construct a new official residence in the 1830s.

Old Government House, New South Wales

In common with many other State Governors in Australia at this time, the Governors of New South Wales also established a 'second' Government House as a country residence, to escape the heat and often unsanitary conditions in the early city settlements. Old Government House at Parramatta was constructed between 1799 and 1820, around 12 miles (20 kilometres) from the centre of Sydney.

Designed by a team from the Colonial Architects of New South Wales including, at different times, John Cliffe Watts, Francis Greenway and Walter Liberty Vernon, Old Government House was built as a Georgian colonial mansion with space for entertaining official visitors. The house was furnished in the style of the 1820s, which has been retained today. The early residence had only two rooms with a central hall, which would have provided a private bedroom for the Governor and a more public living room where visitors could be received. Further rooms and outbuildings were added over time, and extensive renovations in 1815–16 created a new Palladian country house in the English-style.

The settlement of Old Government House, located in extensive grounds that extended to many acres that were known as the 'Government Domain', was chosen because it offered opportunities for growing crops and grazing animals outside of the city, that supplied the Vice-Regal household. These grounds were later transformed into landscaped gardens and orchards. Old Government House was situated at Rose Hill, and the wider township that was established in 1788 became known as Parramatta.

In 1820, Old Government House was badly damaged by a lightning strike and although no physical evidence remains today, considerable repairs were required at the time. By this time, the residence had grown to contain a private suite of rooms for the Governor and his family, plus several rooms for entertaining over two storeys.

Cornfield/Shutterstock 558233008

Above: Old Government House, Parramatta, was an official 'country' residence of the Governors of New South Wales for around 50 years.

In 1822, an observatory was erected in the grounds of Old Government House at the private expense of the newly arrived Governor, Thomas Brisbane, who had brought two astronomers with him and wanted to establish the site as 'the Greenwich of the Southern Hemisphere'. Many astronomical discoveries and measurements were taken from the site over the years, although only the stone piers of the observatory remain today.

Between 1800 and the 1850s, Old Government House was used by at least ten successive Governors of New South Wales, but once the present Government House became established in the centre of Sydney, then it became increasingly difficult to justify the expense and maintenance of a second official residence outside the city. The property was later leased to tenants and also used by several schools, before the former residence was taken over by the National Trust of Australia in 1967 and then later designated as a World Heritage Site by UNESCO in 2010, in recognition of its status in the early settlement and convict history of Australia. The extensive grounds became the Parramatta Park. Today, Old Government House at Parramatta is a heritage museum and is considered to be one of Australia's oldest public buildings.

Government House, New South Wales

The current Government House in New South Wales is located in the heart of Sydney's Royal Botanic Gardens, in the centre of the city and overlooking the harbour. Built between 1837 and 1845, the Gothic-style Victorian residence has the appearance of a small castle. Permission for the construction of a new Government House had been granted in 1836 and the new building was influenced in its architectural approach by the existing Governor's Stables, which had been completed in 1821 (now the Conservatorium of Music located at the main entry gates to Government House).

Government House was designed by Edward Blore, architect to King William IV and Queen Victoria, and followed the style of his other recent work on the British Houses of Parliament, Buckingham Palace and Windsor Castle.

Australia

Building materials of sandstone, marble and cedar wood were sourced from across New South Wales. A ball was held at the house in honour of Queen Victoria's birthday in 1843, even though construction was still underway. The tradition of a ball to celebrate the monarch's birthday was continued by successive Governors for many years.

After years of delay and an escalating budget, Government House was completed in 1845 when Sir George Gipps, 9th Governor of New South Wales, and his family took up residence. It has been the official home of the Governor of New South Wales since then, except for two occasions. During the first period of absence between 1901 and 1913, Government House in Sydney was used by the Governor-General of Australia as their Sydney residence until Admiralty House became available across the harbour. During this time, the Governor of New South Wales lived at a large Victorian property called Cranbrook in Rose Bay, Sydney. The building is now part of Cranbrook School.

The second period of absence was from 1996 to 2013 when disagreements at the state government level over the role of the Governor and their need for an official residence, resulted in the house being unoccupied for around 17 years, although official receptions and functions continued to take place there.

Above left: With its painted ceilings and minstrel's gallery, the Ballroom at Government House in New South Wales is the perfect location for large receptions and investitures.

Above right: The elegant decor continues into the Drawing Room and throughout the official reception rooms at Government House.

Left: Government House in New South Wales was completed in 1845 in the Victorian Gothic-style.

Right: The tropical gardens at Government House provide a beautiful location on the edge of the Royal Botanic Gardens in Sydney.

Today, Government House features a significant collection of Vice-Regal furniture, portraits and ornaments acquired by successive Governors. A magnificent ballroom with its minstrel's gallery features royal portraits and painted ceilings. Further state rooms include a dining room with a table for over 25 guests and a drawing room featuring colonial portraits and modern Australian artworks. The impressive main hall is decorated with the coats of arms of successive Governors, as well as the royal arms and a portrait of Queen Elizabeth II.

The house is often open to the public at the discretion of the current Governor. It also has a garden of around 12 acres (5 hectares) on the edge of the Royal Botanic Gardens, with fantastic views across the harbour and suburbs of Sydney.

Queen Elizabeth II and the Duke of Edinburgh first visited Government House in Sydney in 1954, during their first visit to Australia, and a celebration ball, a garden party and private investiture were all held there at the time. Government House has welcomed many members of the Royal Family, overseas royal families and distinguished guests over the years.

Right: The impressive main hall at Government House in New South Wales decorated with the coats of arms of successive Governors.

Australia

Government House, Queensland

The state of Queensland in the north-east of Australia is one of the most vibrant parts of this vast country. Originally, the state was part of the Colony of New South Wales until the Colony of Queensland was founded on 6 June 1859, named after Queen Victoria, who signed the Letters Patent. However, it was over a month later before word of the newly created colony reached the people of Queensland. In 1901, when the Commonwealth Federation of Australia was founded, Queensland became a State of Australia. The sovereign is represented in the state by the Governor of Queensland.

Old Government House, Queensland

The first official residence, today known as Old Government House, was purpose-built for the Governor in Brisbane, shortly after Queensland achieved independence from New South Wales. The property was located on George Street, overlooking the Botanical Gardens in the city at Gardens Point, and was occupied between 1862 and 1910 by successive Governors. A rare surviving example of the Australian architectural work of Queensland's first Colonial Architect, Charles Tiffin, Old Government House was both a private home and official state office for Sir George Bowen, the state's first Governor.

When the Governor and his family first arrived in Brisbane in 1859, they took up residence at Adelaide House, now the Deanery of St John's Cathedral, which was leased for their use as a temporary Government House, while the construction of Old Government House took place.

A fine colonial building designed in the classical revival style over two floors, the Old Government House saw many royal and official visits. The front half of the property contained the Governor's public and private rooms, while the rear housed the servants' quarters. The residence was constructed from locally sourced materials, including sandstone, Brisbane 'tuff' (stone), red cedar and hoop pine.

The first Vice-Regal Consort, Lady Diamantina Bowen, took a great interest in the gardens around Old Government House, which featured rolling lawns and flower beds on the public side of the building and vegetable gardens at the rear. She collaborated with Walter Hill, Curator of the adjacent Brisbane Botanic Gardens, on a number of projects, including large public events which extended out from the grounds of Old Government House into the Botanic Gardens.

Jeffrey Hyland

Left: Occupied between 1862 and 1910, Old Government House welcomed many royal and official visitors to the state of Queensland.

Right: Today, the former official residence is a heritage-listed building and museum at the heart of the Queensland University of Technology's city campus.

Old Government House was the official residence of the first eleven Governors of Queensland and their families before the Governors moved to Fernberg. The house was added to during this period, with the conversion of the open upper terraces into colonial-style verandahs.

By 1909, the demands on the sovereign's representative in Queensland and the lack of a suitable ballroom for entertaining meant that the once spacious Old Government House was perceived as being too small to function as the Governor's official residence.

Consequently, Old Government House was granted to the newly established University of Queensland as part of the state's 50th anniversary celebrations. As one of Queensland's most significant historical buildings, it was the first in the state to be heritage-listed in 1978 and today remains a heritage-listed building and museum at the heart of the Queensland University of Technology's city campus. In 2006, the university undertook a major three-year restoration of the building and it reopened in 2009 to mark the 150th anniversary of the establishment of Queensland.

Old Government House in Queensland has a unique claim to fame as the origin of the famous Australian cake named the Lamington, made from squares of sponge cake coated in chocolate and desiccated coconut. It is said that the Lamington was invented by the French cook, Armand Gallan, who was working at Old Government House during the time of the Queensland Governor, Lord Lamington between 1896 and 1901.

Fernberg

In 1910, a decision was made to build a new Government House for Queensland in the Victoria Park area of Brisbane. Plans were drawn up and the Governor, Sir William MacGregor, moved temporarily into a large rented property called Fernberg, in the Paddington suburb of the city. In 1911, Fernberg was purchased for £10,000, and although foundations were laid for the new Government House at Victoria Park, it became clear several decades later that it would never be built, so it was decided that Fernberg should become the permanent official residence of the Governor of Queensland.

The history of Fernberg, the name of which means 'distant mountain' in German, goes back much further than its time as Government House. The land on which the house was built was purchased in 1860 by Johann Christian Heussler, a German merchant in search of a warmer climate in Australia. The land is situated about 100 metres above sea level and offers commanding views of the local area. Heussler commissioned a Brisbane architect named Benjamin Backhouse to design a new villa, which was built in 1865, and he remained there until 1871 when financial difficulties forced him to leave.

After several years, successful industrialist and Member of the Queensland Parliament, John Stevenson, bought Fernberg and he commissioned another architect, Richard Gailey, to double the property's size with a wide-ranging programme of building works and additions to the house, which developed into the residence that can largely be seen today. The white Italianate mansion that was created had updated architectural detailing, a new tower over the main entrance and extensive landscaped gardens.

Australia

A central foyer of the house was added during Stevenson's time, with large fireplaces, timber-panelled walls and an intricately carved cedar-wood staircase. The staircase is still dominated by a huge stained-glass window featuring a life-sized portrait of Robert the Bruce, in tribute to Stevenson's Scottish ancestry.

In the 1890s financial crisis that hit Queensland, Stevenson lost his fortune and was forced to sell Fernberg, though he stayed on as a tenant until the early 20th century. In 1910, Fernberg was first rented and then later purchased as the official residence for the Governor of Queensland and thus it became Government House. Many pieces of original furniture from Old Government House were transported to Fernberg and remain in the house today. The prime example is the dining-room suite of yellowwood furniture, including a large table, chairs and sideboards, that were purchased in 1896 for the then Governor, Lord Lamington.

A further building programme in 1937 added a new eastern wing that included a large reception room, later to become the main Drawing Room, and new bedroom suites. It was at this time that the entire exterior of the house was first painted cream and later white, which gives Queensland's Government House its distinctive appearance.

Over the years, further works and restoration have been undertaken at Government House, and a new tennis court, swimming pool, pavilion and porte-cochère entrance have been added. The grounds feature a mixture of formal gardens and natural bushland that contain many of Queensland's native flora and fauna.

Numerous royal visitors have stayed at Government House in Queensland over the years. Queen Elizabeth II and Prince Philip have visited many times, the first time on the Coronation tour of 1953–54. In 1959, Princess Alexandra of Kent made a celebrated tour of

Images below: Government House in Queensland is the setting for many official ceremonies, meetings and events. These often take place in the Governor's Study, the Foyer, the State Dining Room and the Drawing Room.

Official Images: Government House, Queensland

Above: Since the early 20th century, Fernberg in Brisbane has been the official residence of the State Governor of Queensland.

Australia when she came to Brisbane for Queensland's centenary celebrations and to open the Royal National Show.

In the late 1950s and early 1960s, Princess Alice, Countess of Athlone, herself a former occupant of many Government Houses, visited the residence in Brisbane several times when her daughter, Lady May Abel Smith and her son-in-law, Sir Henry Abel Smith lived at Government House when he was the last English-born Governor of Queensland between 1958 and 1966. Since then, all Governors have been Australian and there have been two female Governors of Queensland, with one incumbent, Dame Quentin Bryce, later becoming Australia's first female Governor-General and resident of Government House in Canberra.

Government House in Brisbane is open to the general public on certain open days, usually around Queensland Day (6 June) and during the Brisbane Open House event (normally in October). Public tours, for which bookings are required, are also held on the first Thursday of every month. Otherwise, Government House is a state Vice-Regal residence and is used for hundreds of official and charitable functions throughout the year. The property was listed on the Queensland Heritage Register in 1992 and is recognised as the only remaining substantial residence and original estate of its kind in Brisbane dating from the 1860s.

Right: The stained-glass window featuring a life-sized portrait of Robert the Bruce, which dominates the staircase at Government House.

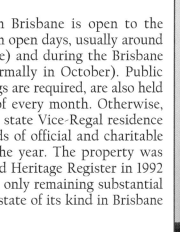

Australia

David O'Keeffe

Government House, Northern Territory

The sparsely populated Northern Territory covers a huge geographic area of the northern Australian mainland of over 500,000 square miles (1.3 million square kilometres) and yet has only a small population of less than 250,000 people. The history of the Northern Territory begins over 40,000 years ago, when indigenous Australians came to dwell in the region with the first European settlers arriving in the 19th century.

Port Darwin was established in 1869 as the main settlement, with the Northern Territory gaining its own position in Australia in 1911 as a territory rather than a state, but with much the same status. The Administrator of the Northern Territory is an official appointed by the Governor-General of Australia to represent the Australian government and they perform a similar role to that of a State Governor. Unlike an Australian State Governor, the Administrator is not the direct representative of the monarch, however as they perform a similar role to State Governors then they are often considered to be the monarch's indirect representative in the Northern Territory.

Government House is the official residence of the Administrator and many official functions for the Northern Territory are held there. The property is one of the oldest European buildings in Darwin and was built between 1870 and 1871. Government House is a mid-Victorian Gothic-style house set in around 3.2 acres (1.3 hectares) of hillside gardens in the centre of Darwin's business district. The chosen site was a hill in the north-west edge of the town of Palmerston (as this area of Darwin was then named).

The building's original structure featured a central hall with stone walls, six bedrooms, a bathroom, pantry and kitchen with the traditional wrap-around verandah typical of houses of that period in Australia. In 1874, a second storey was added, but white ants destroyed it within 12 months – the first of many attacks on the property by the dreaded insects.

In 1878, a new residence known as 'The House of Seven Gables' or The Residency, was designed by John George Knight, a prominent local architect who also became the sixth Government Resident, the name for the local government representative before the first Administrator was appointed in 1912. Made using cypress pine, local porcellanite stone and lime sourced from local coral reefs, the building was completed in 1879.

Above left: The mid-Victorian Gothic-style architecture of Government House in Darwin, Australia gives the residence in the Northern Territory its unique feel.

Right: The dining room features a large Queensland cedar-wood suite of furniture that was specifically designed for Government House, alongside Australian indigenous artworks.

A cyclone caused severe damage to The Residency in 1897 which warranted further renovations and in 1911, when the Northern Territory came under the jurisdiction of the Australian government, more substantial repairs took place.

Dr John Gilruth was appointed as the first Administrator in 1912 and he renamed The Residency as Government House. Additional work on the house included new bathrooms, a servant's block, a modernised kitchen and a rebuilt tennis court. The house has always been a focal point in the history of the Northern Territory and, in December 1918, about 1,000 demonstrators marched to Government House to protest against the Gilruth Administration and demand his resignation in what became known as the Darwin Rebellion.

Images: Government House, Northern Territory official website

In 1937, another cyclone caused widespread damage to the house and later a new bomb shelter was built to double as an office in anticipation of the Second World War. Government House was considered to be at risk at this time, due to the strategic position of Darwin in relation to the battles taking place in the Far East. In 1942, during one of the many bombing raids on Darwin, the office at Government House was destroyed by a direct hit from Japanese aircraft overhead. One of the maids at Government House, Daisy Martin, was killed in the bomb attack, when she was crushed by the rubble and her life is remembered with a plaque in the gardens close to the spot where she died.

One of the worst events to hit Darwin was Cyclone Tracy, a huge tropical cyclone, which passed through the city during Christmas in 1974, causing terrible destruction and loss of life. Government House suffered extensive wind and rain damage, but fortunately remained intact. Six years later, the building was entered on the Register of the National Estate and went on to be declared a Place of Heritage under the *Heritage Conservation Act (Northern Territory)* on 15 March 1996. Extensive refurbishment took place between 2003 and 2010 to restore the house to its 1930s style and to protect it for future generations.

Below left: The main entrance gates to Government House.

Below right: The covered verandahs at Government House, running around the ground floor of the residence, provide an area for receiving guests.

Government House today features many beautiful rooms reflecting the heritage of the Northern Territory. The main guest suite is named in honour of Queen Elizabeth II, who stayed there on 5 October 1982. The bedroom was referred to as the Royal Suite

Australia

throughout the visit, but was later renamed 'The Queen's Bedroom' and now plays host to members of the Royal Family, State Governors and visiting dignitaries.

The drawing room dates from the original 1871 stone structure of the house and is the oldest-known European-style room in Darwin. It is now the main function room in the house and features many fine examples of local Aborigine artworks. The Prince of Wales Room was for many years used as a bedroom suite and in 1988, the Prince and Princess of Wales stayed there during their bicentenary tour of Australia. However, the room has since been returned to its original use as a reception room and today features a specially commissioned carpet made of pure Australian wool, embroidered with the desert rose and the Northern Territory Coat of Arms.

The dining room features a large Queensland cedar-wood dining table, chairs and sideboards that were commissioned by the Administrator's wife, Mrs Hilda Abbott, in 1946. They were the first furniture pieces that were specifically designed for Government House. Crockery by Wedgwood, Christofle silverware and Waterford crystal have also been commissioned for the house at various times and are still used during luncheons and dinners. The verandahs with their original tiles and louvre shutters run around the ground floor of the residence, providing an area for receiving guests away from the strong Australian sunshine.

The gardens at Government House cover about 3.2 acres (1.3 hectares) and were originally developed in the 1890s. The lawn and carriage loop at the front of the house were also laid out at this time and the former was famous for many years as one of only two green lawns in Darwin. The Victorian cannon in the grounds is believed to have belonged to South Australian Surveyor-General George W. Goyder, who arrived in Port Darwin on 5 February 1869. Manufactured in England, the cannon bears the cypher and crown of Queen Victoria.

Government House has endured many challenges over the years, including cyclones, earthquakes, bombing raids and infestations of white ants, but it remains one of the most beautiful and historic buildings in the Northern Territory today.

Left: The main drawing room at Government House is also one of the oldest rooms, dating from the original 1871 stone structure of the house.

Below left and below right: The bright, powder blue-coloured Prince of Wales Room provides a comfortable setting for the Administrator to receive VIP guests to the Northern Territory.

The Residency, Alice Springs

A former Vice-Regal residence dating from the 1920s can be found in Alice Springs in the Northern Territory. Known as The Residency, the building serves as a symbol of the time when Central Australia gained administrative independence from the Northern Australia between 1927 and 1931 under the *North Australia Act*. The boundary for the territory was drawn at a latitude of 20 degrees south and the capital of Central Australia was Stuart Town, which was renamed Alice Springs in 1933.

Construction of The Residency began in 1926 on the corner of Parsons and Hartley Street and was completed the following year. John Charles Cawood was appointed as the first Government Resident of Central Australia in 1926 and the house was designated as his formal residence. It became the centre of the official and social life of the town.

Typical of the Australian architecture of the period, The Residency was designed to protect the inhabitants from the hot and arid climate of the area. Although foundations for the building were laid, the concrete floors were laid directly onto the earth to allow for passive heating and cooling and the concrete bricks used in the building are hollow to provide insulation. One of the main features of the house was a breezeway running through its centre to keep the property cool. Rooms were constructed with side of the breezeway and a wide verandah enclosed the single storey building which today has wooden framed sliding windows with blinds. Further rooms and outbuildings were added in later years.

Cawood was succeeded as Government Resident by Victor Carrington in 1929, who subsequently became the Assistant Administrator and then District Officer when the area became part of the Northern Territory in 1931. The Carrington family occupied the residence until 1942.

Between 1942 and 1945, the Administrator of the Northern Territory temporarily moved the official Vice-Regal residence from Government House in Darwin to The Residency in Alice Springs, along with the Territory's administration due to the threat of bombing in Darwin during the Second World War.

Adam Beck/Copyright free/source Wikipedia

Right: The Residency in Alice Springs is a former Vice-Regal residence dating from the 1920s that has hosted royalty and official visitors over the years.

Australia

Adam Beck/Copyright free/source Wikipedia

The house returned to its role as the District Officer's residence following the war and it was occupied by various holders of the position and their families until 1973 when it was acquired by the Museums and Art Galleries of the Northern Territory.

Over the years, The Residency in Alice Springs played host to several members of the Royal Family. In 1946, Prince Henry, Duke of Gloucester and his wife, Prince Alice, Duchess of Gloucester visited Alice Springs and stayed at The Residency when the Duke was Governor-General of Australia between 1945 to 1947.

The most important royal visit came from 14 to 16 March 1963 when Queen Elizabeth II and Prince Philip, Duke of Edinburgh toured Alice Springs and stayed for two nights at The Residency. Their hosts were District Officer, Daniel Conway and his wife Jillna who had prepared for the royal visit with extensive renovations to the residence including a new roof, air conditioning and the installation of two new bathrooms. Part of the verandah near to The Queen's bedroom was designated as a private area for the royal couple. During this trip to Alice Springs, they toured the headquarters of the famous Royal Flying Doctor Service of Australia and The Queen broadcast a message to citizens over the radio.

However, it was not Prince Philip's first visit to the Royal Flying Doctor Service or to The Residency as he had stayed there for two nights in November 1956 during a visit to Alice Springs on route to opening the Olympic Games in Melbourne on behalf of The Queen. The Prince also visited the ANZAC Oval to meet local school children playing various sports and went to the Connellan Airways aerodrome.

Above left and below: The Residency is today used as a heritage museum and community centre.

The Prince of Wales and Diana, Princess of Wales came to The Residency for a reception during their visit to Alice Springs in March 1983. Their arrival in Alice Springs marked the start of their six-week tour of Australia and New Zealand. They were accompanied by a 10-month old Prince William, although the tiny Prince continued his journey with his nanny to a remote farm in New South Wales, while his parents spent four days in Alice Springs. The royal couple had a busy schedule that included visits to Yulara and Uluru (Ayers Rock), the Alice Springs School of the Air and to Tennant Creek.

The Residency is now administered by Heritage Alice Springs and the former residence is used for community events, exhibitions and a local tourist attraction.

Adam Beck/Copyright free/source Wikipedia

Government House, South Australia

The state of South Australia has a population of under 2 million people, with more than 75% living in or around the state capital of Adelaide. The state is notable for sharing a land border with all of the other mainland Australian states. South Australia was founded in 1836 and is unique in being settled by Europeans to establish a province in Australia rather than for use as a convict settlement. The Crown is represented by a Governor in South Australia and they reside in central Adelaide in the oldest current Government House in the country, parts of which date from 1840.

The first Government House in South Australia, known as the 'Government Hut', was a temporary construction of timber, wattle and daub walls, covered by a thatched roof. Unsuitable for long-term habitation, plans were drawn up by an English architect, Edward O'Brien, for a new stone-built residence for the Governor with a budget not exceeding £5,000. The plans were modified by another early settler, George Strickland Kingston, and although the costs increased further to £7,000, building contractors Messrs East and Breeze were appointed to start the work.

The earliest part of Government House in Adelaide to be built was the present-day East Wing, which was completed and occupied in May 1840. This part of the house contains many of the formal rooms, including the drawing room, morning room and dining room with three bedrooms, a dressing room and two small servants' rooms upstairs. Kitchens and further rooms were originally located in separate adjacent buildings.

Above and right: The grounds of Government House cover almost 14 acres (6 hectares) in central Adelaide and are used for official functions, such as garden parties or military parades.

Australia

In 1855, as the state's prosperity increased with the discovery of copper and gold, Government House was further extended by contractors English and Brown with an additional wing to create a large Victorian residence fit for the monarch's Vice-Regal representative in South Australia. New rooms included the small drawing room, the south-facing entrance hall, the large ballroom, a formal dining room and further bedrooms at a cost of £8,200, despite the objections of the then Governor, Sir Henry Fox Young, who had wanted to explore the option of constructing a new property near to the River Torrens.

The first royal visitor to Government House in Adelaide was Queen Victoria's son, Prince Alfred, Duke of Edinburgh, who arrived in October 1867 during his extensive tour of Australia. More additions to the house were made in the 1860s and 1870s that turned Government House into a large formal residence with vast formal rooms for state occasions. This included the creation of a new conservatory (now the library), a billiard room and porter's hall, and new furniture and repairs were added at an estimated cost of around £4,000. In 1874, the first guard room was demolished and the western boundary of the property was moved around seven metres to the east, to provide for the widening of King William Road, and a new west wall was built. Small cottages were built in the grounds in the 20th century for use as staff accommodation.

Above left: The Governor's Study features a rectangular pedestal desk that dates from the 1868 inventory of furniture in the house. The room is used for official business and meetings with staff.

Above right: The main entrance gate to Government House in Adelaide.

Left: First installed to commemorate the visit of the Duke and Duchess of Cornwall and York in 1901, the stained-glass 'Federation Windows' in the State Ballroom are one of the most striking features of Government House.

Jeffrey Hyland

Right: The East Wing is the earliest part of Government House, which was completed in May 1840.

Notable features of the State Ballroom at Government House today are the alcove, dais and stained-glass windows installed by the Governor, Lord Tennyson, on the occasion of the visit of the Duke and Duchess of Cornwall and York (later King George V and Queen Mary), in 1901, during their Federation tour of Australia. The stained glass 'Federation Windows' were designed and made by E. F. Troy of Adelaide and feature several royal coats of arms and cyphers, E&A for King Edward VII and Queen Alexandra, G&V for the Duke and Duchess of Cornwall and York, Lord Tennyson's coat of arms, the coat of arms of South Australia, and the date of the state's foundation, 1836. Later additions to the stained-glass collection include Queen Elizabeth II's coat of arms to commemorate her first visit to Adelaide in 1954 and a modern-design Federation centenary window on the main staircase, which was installed in 2001. All of the main chandeliers in Government House are crystal and were made by Richardson's of Stourbridge in England, some time during the 1860s, before being carefully shipped to Australia.

Below left: A rare photograph on display at Government House which shows the Duke and Duchess of Cornwall and York leaving the East Wing entrance during their 1901 visit to South Australia.

There have been many royal visits to Government House in South Australia over the years. Queen Elizabeth II and the Duke of Edinburgh have been welcomed eight times and in anticipation of their visit to Adelaide in the 1970s, some of the rooms on the first floor of the original East Wing were modernised to form a separate suite, including two bedrooms, a sitting room and staff rooms for the royal party.

Below right: This painting by Charles Crampton dates from 1889 and depicts a garden party in the grounds of Government House.

Most of the artworks on display at Government House are on loan from the Art Gallery of South Australia. Among the Government House collection is a rare painting titled *Garden Party at Government House*, which was completed by Charles Crampton in 1889 and hangs in the State Entrance.

Jeffrey Hyland

Jeffrey Hyland

Australia

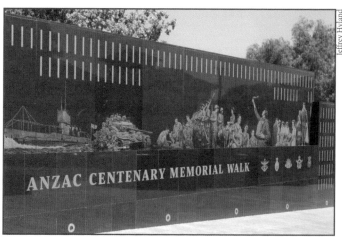

Other rare historical artefacts at Government House are two memorial plaques that were sent to South Australia from London to mark the deaths of Queen Victoria in 1901 and King Edward VII in 1910. Both of which were hung on the gates of the official residence to announce the sovereigns' deaths to the public.

In 2016, the ANZAC Centenary Memorial Walk was opened by the then Governor of South Australia, Hieu Van Le, which runs along the eastern side of Government House, along Kintore Avenue. The public memorial walk commemorates over 102,000 service personnel from South Australia who made the ultimate sacrifice in military conflicts around the world.

Today, Government House hosts receptions, investitures and garden parties on behalf of South Australia, and is the office and official residence of the Governor. Open days for visitors are held each year.

Images below: The state rooms include the Ballroom, the State Dining Room and the Morning Room. The Morning Room is said to be Queen Elizabeth II's favourite room at the residence and brass plaques on the door commemorate notable royal visitors.

Old Government House, South Australia

Due to the extreme heat of South Australia, in the 19th century, the Governor of South Australia and his family would escape the hot, dusty summers and their main residence in the Adelaide Plains to a second official home located in the Adelaide Hills, around 7 miles (11 kilometres) south of the city centre.

The first of these 'summer' residences was Old Government House at Belair National Park, which was in use between 1860 and 1880. In around 1840, the then Governor directed that an area of the Adelaide Hills in the Upper Sturt Valley would be set aside for the housing and breeding of livestock and horses for the state's use, and a designated Government Farm was established. A number of buildings and small cottages were built there as the estate became more widely used.

Between 1856 and 1858, with the state's economy growing, the Governor, Sir Richard MacDonnell, sought another property outside of the city and the South Australia Government approved the construction of Old Government House as a summer residence, in the area of the Government Farm. It was built from local sandstone from a quarry still visible from the house today, with the red-brick additions sourced from the local Blackwood brickworks and a native-timber shingle roof.

Although Old Government House was relatively small compared to other state residences, the addition of a bay window with a turret and flagpole distinguished the house from other local buildings and gave it a Vice-Regal air. It was designed by the Colonial Architect, Edward Hamilton, with assistance from R. A. Hyndman and G. K. Soward, while Charles Farr was chosen as the chief builder. When Old Government House was completed in 1860, it contained two main rooms (a dining room and a bedroom), a small office, bathroom, dressing room and

Above right and right: Old Government House at Belair National Park was used as a summer residence by the Governors of South Australia between 1860 and 1880.

Australia

Above images: The interior of Old Government House has been restored with period furniture and Victorian wallpaper.

a generous underground cellar. The large five-sided bay window in the dining room has French-style doors which open out onto the wide, tiled terrace, overlooking the gardens and huge eucalyptus trees. The residence's indoor plunge-pool, containing water from a local spring, was reportedly the first in South Australia. The total cost of the building was said to be around £1,600, a substantial sum for the time.

Old Government House was the summer home of three Governors of South Australia from 1860 to 1880. It was mainly used by the Governors for shooting weekends and horseback riding, as the terrain and bushlands were said to be harsh. The property was later superseded by a larger summer residence at Marble Hill.

Old Government House was then used by the state's Survey Department for the manufacture of rabbit poison, as the animals were devastating the local crops and vegetation. The house was transferred to the Department of Woods and Forests Nursery, before being taken over by the National Parks and Wildlife Reserves in 1961. The area around Government Farm was designated as the Belair National Park, with other parts being developed as the suburbs of Glenalta and Monalta in the housing boom of the mid-20th century.

Old Government House was opened as a museum in 1961 and extensive renovations took place in the 1970s and again in 2002–03, which restored the building to its previous grandeur. Although the original furniture of the property was no longer in place, many period furnishings in the mid-Victorian style and artworks were restored to the house. The former summer residence is today a tourist attraction and is open to the public on selected days, administered by the voluntary group, Friends of Old Government House.

Marble Hill, South Australia

In 1880, Old Government House was given up in favour of a much bigger summer home for the Governors of South Australia at Marble Hill near Norton Summit, which was in use for nearly 75 years. The residence was around 12 miles (20 kilometres) east of Adelaide, in an area that had been designated as a government reserve in 1878.

The building at Marble Hill took two years to construct and ran hugely over budget, but the grandeur of the house and its suitability for grand entertaining persuaded the government to complete the construction. The designing architect, William McMinn, had originally planned a residence of over 40 rooms, although only 26

Left: The indoor plunge-pool at Old Government House was reportedly the first example of its kind constructed in South Australia and the spring water was sourced from within Belair National Park.

Right: The original Old Government House in Belair National Park was opened as a museum in 1961 and today is a tourist attraction that is open to the public on selected days.

were completed. The house was designed in the Victorian Gothic-revival style, with a huge tower and verandahs on three sides. The interior was notable for its imposing staircase of kauri pine and blackwood.

All 15 State Governors from 1880 to 1955 stayed at the Vice-Regal summer residence at Marble Hill and a number of

distinguished guests were entertained there, including the Duke and Duchess of Cornwall and York who stayed at the house in 1901. Another notable visitor was Lady Baden-Powell in her capacity as World Chief Guide, who was welcomed to Marble Hill during her 1948 trip to Australia.

Unfortunately, the residence of Marble Hill was located at the peak of a steep, densely wooded ridge that was regularly affected by bushfires, triggered by the extreme heat. Consequently, there were many incidents of bushfires close to the house over the years.

In January 1955, the Marble Hill property was completely destroyed in the Black Sunday bushfires that spread rapidly across the area. The then Governor, Sir Robert George and his family were staying there at the time and struggled with their guests and staff to save the house. They endured a terrible ordeal, although fortunately all of those in the building at the time survived the fire. Sadly, the Vice-Regal family lost all of their possessions, as they had been transferred to Marble Hill whilst the main Government House in central Adelaide was undergoing restoration, following damage suffered in the earthquake of 1954. Due to the huge cost of reconstruction, the Government of South Australia announced that Marble Hill would not be rebuilt and, since 1955, the Governor of South Australia has not been provided with a summer residence.

The ruins of the house and estate at Marble Hill were managed by the National Trust of South Australia (1967 to 1992), the Department for Environment and Heritage (1992 to 2009) and have subsequently been sold to a private developer, who hopes to restore the former summer residence to its original glory and has already started to hold events in the original stable block and within the grounds of the estate.

Right: Two rare photographs on display at Government House in central Adelaide showing the Vice-Regal residence at Marble Hill before and after the devastating bushfire that destroyed the house in 1955.

Australia

Government House, Tasmania

Tasmania is an island state off the south coast of Australia, comprising the main island of 24,000 square miles (64,500 kilometres) and 334 smaller islands. With a population of just over 500,000 people, Tasmania has a diverse landscape of national parks and World Heritage Sites. Tasmania was settled by Europeans in the early 19th century and the British established a penal colony there in 1803. It was recognised as a self-governing state in 1825 under the name of 'Van Diemen's Land'. However, the name of Tasmania was later established in 1855.

The monarch is represented in the state by the Governor of Tasmania and their official Vice-Regal residence is Government House in the capital city of Hobart. It is believed that Tasmania's first official dwelling was a canvas tent at Sullivan's Cove on the west bank of the River Derwent, which was occupied by the Lieutenant-Governor from early settlement until a small thatched cottage was built near to what became the entrance to the Town Hall in Hobart. The first brick-built Government House in Tasmania was constructed around 1807 and was added to several times over the years. However, the house was deemed unsuitable for official entertaining and a new residence was sought.

Today's Government House in Tasmania occupies a site at Pavilion Point near to the Royal Tasmanian Botanical Gardens and construction began in 1853. The sandstone structure was built with stone from quarries within the grounds (now ornamental ponds) and local timbers along with Welsh slate for the roof.

Above: This rare historic image from 1868 shows Prince Alfred, Duke of Edinburgh, and his entourage visiting Government House in Tasmania during his 1867–68 tour of Australia.

This page images: The building's architecture is neo-Gothic, which was popular in early Victorian times. At the time of its construction, Tasmania's Government House was one of the largest Vice-Regal residences in Australia.

Below: The main entrance hall at Government House.

Government House was completed in 1857 and Sir Henry Fox Young was the first Governor to live in the residence from January 1858. The house has remained largely unchanged since then, apart from the rebuilding of the conservatory in the 1990s.

Government House was designed by the colonial architect, William Porden Kay, and is a fine example of early Victorian neo-Gothic, featuring sandstone chimney pots and bas-relief sculptures. The clock in the main tower at Government House was the first public clock in Tasmania and was originally erected in the tower of St David's Church in Hobart, which later became the Cathedral Church of St David. The main supporting beam for the clock and flagpole was salvaged from the convict transport ship, the *George III*, which was shipwrecked in the D'Entrecasteaux Channel off Tasmania in 1835 with the loss of 134 lives.

Australia

The interior of the residence has a large number of beautifully decorated formal rooms used for official entertaining. The dining room contains painted ceiling panels featuring the arms of England, Scotland and Ireland, and a large-leaved table made of cedar wood from New South Wales that can seat up to 34 guests.

One of the rooms in the house is called the 'French Room' in honour of its hand-painted wallpaper and furniture in the French Empire-style. The ballroom features a local Tasmanian wood floor made of huon pine (also known as Macquarie pine) and three mirrors that were the largest in the Southern Hemisphere when first installed. The ballroom also has three huge crystal chandeliers, each comprising over 4,000 pieces of crystal, and the crests of many of the former Governors of Tasmania line the walls.

In the 19th century, furniture was specially ordered from London furniture makers, Trollope and Sons, to be shipped out to Government House from England. Much of the furniture is still in use today.

Above left and above right: Government House contains a 'French Room' decorated with hand-painted wallpaper and furniture in the French Empire-style.

Below left: The formal dining room at Government House is the setting for State dinners and lunches.

Below right: The Ballroom at Government House.

Images: Courtesy of Government House, Tasmania

Right and below right: The decor of the drawing room at Government House reflects the Victorian affection for elaborate decoration and rich colours. Small receptions, investitures and awards presentations are held in this room today.

The extensive grounds of Government House stretch across 37 acres (15 hectares) of formal Victorian gardens and paddocks that were laid out in the 1850s and 1860s by landscape gardener, William Thomas. Some of the oak trees on the estate predate the house, having been planted in the 1840s, and many royal visitors have planted trees that are marked by brass plaques. Cattle, that belong to a local farming school, can often be seen grazing in the paddocks in front of Government House.

Queen Elizabeth II and Prince Philip made their first royal visit to Tasmania in 1954 and they have returned several times, including in 1977 and 1988. The Queen's uncle, Prince Henry, Duke of Gloucester, and his wife, Princess Alice, Duchess of Gloucester, themselves a former Vice-Regal couple when the Duke was Governor-General of Australia in the 1940s, visited Tasmania again in 1965 when the Duke opened the new Tasman Bridge in Hobart. Many members of the Royal Family have visited Government House and it also played host to Crown Prince Frederik and Crown Princess Mary of Denmark, when they planted two trees in the grounds during a visit to the Australian-born Princess's homeland in 2005.

Australia

Government House, Victoria

The Australian state of Victoria initially formed part of the Colony of New South Wales. It was named in honour of Queen Victoria, the monarch when Victoria was established as a state in 1851. Melbourne became the largest city and state capital.

At the heart of Melbourne's Royal Botanic Gardens is the impressive Government House of Victoria. Built on the highest point of the Royal Botanic Gardens to the south of the Yarra River, this Vice-Regal residence has a story that reflects the many changes in Australia's constitutional history over the years. Government House is the official residence of the Governor of Victoria today.

The concept of a Government House as a formal home for the Governor was first conceived in the 1840s and 1850s under the first Lieutenant-Governor of Victoria, Charles La Trobe, who set aside a plot of land for the purpose. At the time, the first Government House in Victoria was a prefabricated wooden building brought from England in 1839 by La Trobe and erected on his estate 'Jolimont', near to the present-day Melbourne Cricket Ground. It was the official residence until 1854 and today, La Trobe's Cottage has been partly reconstructed at a nearby location as one of Victoria's oldest surviving buildings.

Between 1854 and 1874, a lease was taken out on Toorak House in Melbourne as the state home of the Governor until a permanent Government House was built. The property is now owned by the Swedish Church and is one of the only surviving houses to be built prior to the discovery of gold in Victoria.

It was not until the 1870s that the Inspector-General of the Public Works Department, William Wardell, was commissioned to draw up plans for a fine Vice-Regal

Above: Government House is located in the Royal Botanic Gardens Victoria, which was founded in 1846, when land was reserved on the south side of the Yarra River. It extends across 94 acres (38 hectares) of formal and informal gardens, lakes and lawns.

residence as the new Government House. Along with his colleagues, J. J. Clarke and Peter Kerr, Wardell designed an Italianate building said to take its inspiration from the Queen-Empress Victoria's summer home, Osborne House, located on the Isle of Wight off the English south coast, with a similar 44-metre high belvedere tower. The extravagant style of the property was said to reflect the prosperous economy in Victoria due to the 'gold rush' in the second half of the 19th century.

A further residence – 'Bishopscourt' in East Melbourne – was rented between 1874 and 1876 to accommodate the Governor until the new home was completed. This house was occupied by the Bishop of Melbourne, who was leaving the city on an extended sabbatical overseas, and so the property was vacant. Today, Bishopscourt has returned to being the official residence of the Anglican Archbishop of Melbourne.

Victoria's Government House in Melbourne was finally completed between 1872 and 1876, and in total, its construction and the purchase of furnishings cost around £200,000, a huge sum at the time. Sir George Bowen, Governor of Victoria from 1873 to 1879 became the first resident in 1876. Only 25 years later, the house was to become the formal home of the first Governor-General of Australia, the Earl of Hopetoun, in 1901. It was not the Earl of Hopetoun's first time at Government House, as he had served as Governor of Victoria between 1889 and 1895 and so was a previous occupant.

In 1901, Melbourne had become the interim federal capital city of the newly founded Commonwealth of Australia, and Government House in Melbourne would become the official residence of the monarch's national Vice-Regal representative, the Governor-General of Australia, for almost 30 years.

The establishment of the Commonwealth of Australia in 1901 was marked by the first visit to the country by a future monarch. The Duke and Duchess of Cornwall and York (later King George V and Queen Mary) stayed at Government House for an extensive programme

Australia

Left: One of the many smaller rooms at Government House, that is used for private audiences with the Governor.

Chris Phutully

of engagements. The main purpose of their tour was to open the first Federal Parliament of Australia on 9th May 1901, on behalf of the new King Edward VII. It was noted that the Duchess and her ladies-in-waiting were dressed in black the entire time as the royal court was still in mourning for the death of Queen Victoria earlier in the year.

During the First World War, Government House was used by the Australian Red Cross as a packing and distribution base as part of the war effort. Government House was to be the home for eight successive Governors-General of Australia until the late 1920s, when the newly built city of Canberra was declared as the new capital of Australia. The Governor-General of the time, Lord Stonehaven, moved to the new official residence in Canberra in 1927, leaving Victoria's Government House empty.

Between 1901 and 1931, the State Governors of Victoria lived at a fine Victorian mansion called Stonington, in another suburb of Melbourne, which is now a private residence.

David O'Keeffe

Left: The grand staircase at Government House leads to the upper floors and the private apartments of the State Governor.

Right: The original
conservatory at Government
House is one of the most
beautiful rooms in the
residence and it offers
fantastic views across the
city of Melbourne.

Following the departure of the Governor-General of Australia, Government House in Victoria was left largely unoccupied due to the financial depression that gripped the country. Between 1931 and 1933, the house was temporarily provided to Melbourne Girls' High School and its 756 students, as their original premises were in disrepair. Minor alterations were made to the residence and the Ballroom became the school's assembly hall. In 1933, the school moved to West Melbourne and was later renamed MacRobertson Girls' High School.

In 1934, Government House reverted to its original role as the State Governor's official residence and has remained so ever since. Today it is a handsome Italianate building divided into three main wings – the state rooms, the Ballroom and the private residence. There are said to be over 240 rooms across the entire estate, and it is believed to be one of the largest remaining Government Houses in the Commonwealth.

The main entrance to the state rooms is dominated by the 32-metre entrance hall and its painting of Queen Elizabeth II. The portrait of The Queen wearing a yellow dress (coincidentally the colour of the Governor of Victoria's flag) was painted by Brian Dunlop in 1984 to mark the Sesquicentenary of the State of Victoria. It is said to be one of The Queen's favourite portraits.

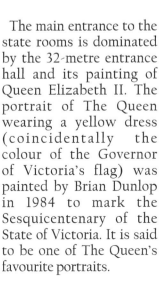

Right: Australian artist,
Brian Dunlop often painted
portraits on commission,
notably the sesquicentenary
portrait of The Queen,
which is on loan from the
National Gallery of Victoria,
Melbourne.

Australia

Left: During an open day at Government House, visitors admire the State Dining Room with its magnificent dining suite.

Just off the main hall is one of the most used rooms in the house, the formal State Drawing room. Light, spacious and featuring some of the finest Australian furniture by the Melbourne firm of George Thwaites and Sons, as well as paintings from the National Gallery of Victoria, the room is used by the Governor for receptions and music recitals.

The adjoining conservatory adds extra light to the room and expresses the widely held Victorian theme of connecting with nature. There are two photographs in the corner of the room showing the young Duke and Duchess of Cornwall and York in the same conservatory on their 1901 visit to Government House.

The State Dining Room is a large formal room used for entertaining on a grand scale. The dining table was made from Spanish mahogany and Australian red cedar by the local firm of James McEwan and Company, and comfortably seats over 50 people. The walls are hung with portraits of former reigning kings and queens – Queen Victoria, King Edward VII and Queen Alexandra, King George V and Queen Mary and King George VI and Queen Elizabeth.

At the south end of the house is a carriage entrance to the huge State Ballroom. This small vestibule allowed guests to arrive for functions without disturbing the residents of

the main house. The State Ballroom itself is an impressive 42 metres long and occupies an entire wing of the building. At the time that Government House was built in the 1870s, it was reputed to be the biggest ballroom in the entire British Empire and it is said to be even larger than the State Ballroom at Buckingham Palace. It is rumoured that when Queen Victoria was shown the plans for the new Government House in Victoria, she

disapproved of the size of the ballroom and instructed that a smaller room be designed. However, by the time The Queen's disapproval had been communicated to the architects in Melbourne, many thousands of miles away, the house and its ballroom had already been built.

The peacock-blue decor of the ballroom reflects the heraldic family colours of the first Governor-General of Australia, Lord Hopetoun, and the impressive crystal chandeliers were made by Ostlers of Birmingham, England. The blue state throne at the head of the room is only occupied by the sovereign or their representative in Victoria, the Governor. Today, the State Ballroom is used for large receptions, investitures and state balls, such as the Cup Eve ball before the famous Melbourne Cup horse race.

Approached by a third entrance, the private wing of Government House is used by the Governor of Victoria as their official home. The hallway gives access to the first floor via the grand staircase, and the Governor's rooms include a dining room, drawing room and their official study.

The private apartments also house the royal suite where members of the Royal Family stay during official visits to Victoria. There have been a large number of royal guests, from the early stay of the Prince of Wales (later the Duke of Windsor) in 1920 to numerous visits by Queen Elizabeth II and the Duke of Edinburgh and members of the present Royal Family over many years.

The residence hosts a wide range of official functions for the state of Victoria and it is often open to the public on Australia Day and other special occasions.

Today, Government House is recognised as one of the finest examples of Italianate architecture in Australia and, towering above the Royal Botanic Gardens in the centre of the city, is a familiar sight to the residents of Melbourne.

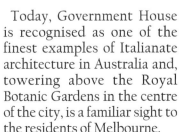

Above right and right: The State Ballroom features the heraldic arms of the Crown and a blue state throne at the head of the room.

Australia

Government House, Western Australia

The largest of the Australian states, Western Australia is also one of the most sparsely populated, with most of the 2.6 million population living in the south-west corner in and around Perth, the state capital.

One of the first settlements by the British in the area was a military garrison at Albany in the 1820s, before the establishment of the Swan River Colony in 1829 with the city of Perth as its capital.

The monarch is represented by the Governor of Western Australia and their official residence is Government House. The present Government House, in the centre of Perth, has been in use since 1863, although it replaced a former Vice-Regal home on the same site.

The first Lieutenant-Governor (later Governor) of Western Australia, Captain Sir James Stirling, RN, oversaw the construction of the first permanent Government House in 1834 in Stirling Gardens, a small public park in Perth. The plans for the building were drawn up by civil engineer, Henry Reveley, who had arrived in Western Australia in 1829. A Georgian residence, this Government House was unfortunately insufficient for the Vice-Regal functions that were required and it suffered from defects from the start, including

Above left and below: Government House in Perth has been the official residence of successive Governors of Western Australia since 1863.

Images: Courtesy of Government House, Western Australia

Right: The main entrance to Government House is dominated by the 'Baronial Hall' with its dramatic stained-glass windows and black-and-white floor.

leaking roofs and a termite infestation. Successive Governors battled with the property to keep it from falling down and faced constant bills for repairs. Often, the Governor and their families resided in other houses during the winter months.

In September 1858, after lobbying by the fifth Governor, Arthur Edward Kennedy, funding was eventually granted for the construction of a new official residence. Lieutenant Colonel E. Henderson, Comptroller of Convicts, was engaged to design the second permanent Government House in Perth, which remains in use today. Henderson worked with James

Australia

Manning, Clerk of Works, and Richard Roach Jewell, Colonial Clerk of Public Works, and together they oversaw a team of convict labour. However, costs for the new property ran over budget and it took much longer than expected, so that the next Governor, John Stephen Hampton, and his family were the first to occupy the house in 1863, prior to its eventual completion in 1864.

The new Government House for Western Australia was modelled on a mixture of Jacobean and Gothic architecture, popular in Victorian times, with fine stonework, turrets and gables. Although it is not the largest Government House in Australia, the substantial residence has 16 large reception rooms on the ground floor and 25 rooms on the first floor.

A new banqueting hall was constructed in anticipation of the first royal visit to Western Australia by Prince Alfred, Duke of Edinburgh, in 1869. Further additions to the house were made at the end of the 19th century, with a new ballroom, dining room and billiard room (now the Executive Council Room), which were designed by government architect, Hillson Beasley.

One of the most imposing rooms is the impressive 'Baronial Hall' at the main entrance, which has a dramatic black-and-white floor made from Welsh slate and stone that was imported from Great Britain in the 1860s. The baronial theme continues in the stained-glass window and the oak-beamed ceiling featuring royal arms and shields.

The tradition of planting trees in the grounds of Government House to commemorate royal visits began in 1920, when the Prince of Wales (later King Edward VIII) planted a kauri tree in the gardens. This was followed by the Duke and Duchess of York (later King George VI and Queen Elizabeth), who planted a gum tree and a weeping fig while visiting Perth in 1927, after attending the opening of the first Parliament House in Canberra.

Below: The Dining Room was constructed between 1897 and 1899 and it features a decorative ceiling of Australian Jarrah hardwood.

Images Courtesy of Government House, Western Australia

Right: The Drawing Room at Government House is where the Governor of Western Australia receives visitors and holds small meetings with community leaders and visiting dignitaries.

Images: Courtesy of Government House, Western Australia

Queen Elizabeth II and Prince Philip first visited Western Australia during their Australia tour in 1954, the first of many trips to the state, with the most recent in October 2011, when The Queen travelled to Perth to attend the Commonwealth Heads of Government Meeting. Many members of the Royal Family have also been made welcome at Government House.

As one of the most important residences in Western Australia, Government House in Perth has been listed on the Western Australian Register of Heritage Places and been subject to a conservation plan since the 1990s, which continues a programme of restoration and conservation to the house and its 7.9 acres (3.2 hectares) of gardens to this day.

Right: The Gallery Corridor features many portraits of the Royal Family and several photographs of Governors' wives.

Australia

The Residency, Albany

A former Vice-Regal residence can be found in Albany in Western Australia. Located south-east of Perth, Albany is the oldest colonial settlement in Western Australia and was founded on 21 January 1827 when British explorer, Major Edmund Lockyer arrived to settle the area. As such it is the location for some of the state's oldest colonial buildings.

The Residency is located on a hill overlooking Princess Royal Harbour, named after Princess Charlotte Augusta Matilda, the first daughter and fourth child of King George III.

The single-storey building was originally constructed in 1850 and it served as a store and office depot for the nearby Albany Convict Gaol. It was constructed as one main room, but three further rooms were added. In 1872, the depot was closed, and the building was renovated with the addition of seven more rooms and a verandah in preparation for its new role as the Governor's Residence. From 1873 to 1953, the building was the official residence and office for the local Administrator for the area, known as the Government Resident until 1901 and later as the Resident Magistrate. The Residency hosted official events, balls and other social events.

Prince George of Wales (later King George V) is said to have spent his sixteenth birthday at The Residency with his older brother, Prince Albert Victor of Wales in 1881 when they were on a naval tour and their ship, HMS *Bacchante*, broke its rudder during a storm.

In 1936, the Major Lockyer Memorial was erected in the grounds between The Residency and the harbour. From 1953 to 1970, the building had various other uses including a school hostel, a sea scout headquarters, a naval depot and a training facility. In 1975, the building was renovated, and it reopened as the Residency Museum, part of the Western Australian Museum.

Queen Elizabeth II and the Duke of Edinburgh visited the site of The Residency in March 1977 to officially open the Lockyer Memorial as part of the 150th anniversary of the first British settlement in Western Australia.

The Residency Museum, also referred to as the Museum of the Great Southern, is today a heritage museum with galleries displaying with stories from Aboriginal and Wadjella (non-Aboriginal) histories and information about regional biodiversity.

Below: The Residency was a Vice-Regal residence in Albany, Western Australia between 1873 and 1953. Today, it is a heritage site and museum.

Right: The Rocks in Albany, Western Australia was used as a Vice-Regal residence and summer home between 1912 and 1937. Today, it is a private residence.

Image: HughesDarren/Creative Commons Attribution license/Wikipedia

The Rocks, Albany

Another historic former Vice-Regal residence in Albany in Western Australia is The Rocks, also referred to as Government House or Government Cottage.

The property is a grand two-storey residence with federation filigree-style architecture from the late 19th century and verandahs on the ground and first floors. It has seven bedrooms, eight bathrooms, a billiard room and a library with Victorian ceilings and jarrah-wood floorboards. The house is located in a large garden on the side of Mount Melville and overlooks the Princess Royal Harbour.

The building was constructed in 1882 for a prominent local businessman, William Grills Knight, who later served as Mayor of the City of Albany from 1886 to 1888. The Knight family remained at the property until 1910 when the property changed hands several times.

In 1912, the Government of Western Australia bought the property to be used as a summer residence for Vice-Regal dignitaries. During the First World War and up until 1921, the house was used as a convalescent home for Australian wounded servicemen and it was again used as a Vice-Regal residence until 1937.

The building was utilised as a school, maternity and general hospitals and during the Second World War, it was again used as a hospital for injured servicemen. In the following years, the property again regularly changed ownership and was used as a private hospital and then a hostel for girls attending Albany Senior High School. Today it is a private home and is used as a boutique hotel.

The building was classified by the National Trust in 1977 and placed on the National Estate register in 1980 in recognition of its importance as an example of the architecture typical of Albany of the late 19th century and its Vice-Regal history.

Australia

Government House, Norfolk Island

Norfolk Island is a small island in the Pacific Ocean located between Australia and New Zealand and it has the status of an External Territory of Australia. It was first settled by Polynesians but was unpopulated for many years until the arrival of the British in 1788. The island served as a convict penal settlement until 1855 when it was largely abandoned. A second settlement began in 1856, when 194 descendants of the Tahitians and the HMS *Bounty* mutineers were resettled from the Pitcairn Islands in the South Pacific Ocean, which had become too small for the growing population. Today, Norfolk Island has a population of just under 2,000 people.

Norfolk Island came under the jurisdiction of first New South Wales and then Tasmania in the 19th and 20th centuries, before it formally joined Australia with the passing of the *Norfolk Island Act 1913*. From 1914, it was administered as an external territory. Between 1979 and 2016, the island had its own self-government with an elected Legislature, but since this period Norfolk Island has been under the direct jurisdiction of the Australian federal government, although there is a movement for self-governance. During its history, the Crown has been represented in Norfolk Island by a succession of Lieutenant-Governors, Commandants, Chief Magistrates and Administrators, who have undertaken similar duties to that of a State Governor. Since its construction in 1829, Government House, Norfolk Island has been the official residence of the Crown's representative.

The present Government House incorporates part of an 1804 property (the third official residence built on the island). It was left unoccupied in 1855 but was repaired in 1862 and used as a school, then as a house for visiting officials and later for the island's magistrates. Since 1913, it has been home to successive Administrators of Norfolk Island. The property contains 25 rooms set around four internal courtyards, with a verandah around three sides of the building. Major reconstruction and renovation work was undertaken between 1976 and 1978, and again in 2001 to ensure the structure remained intact. A number of rooms have been restored to their original 1830s style and to preserve the fine Georgian architecture.

Notable features of the residence include many fine artworks and furniture left by successive Administrators, with many pieces made from local materials or featuring aspects of the island's history, such as the 1856 painting by John Allcot of the *Morayshire*, one of the ships that brought the settlers from the Pitcairn Islands to Norfolk Island in 1856. The 6-metre long dining table

Peter Cousins

Above: Government House in Norfolk Island incorporates part of an 1804 residence that was later left unoccupied before being used as a school and official home for the local magistrates. Since 1913, it has been used by successive Administrators of Norfolk Island.

of Australian cedar is believed to be the only piece of original furniture in the house. It was first used in the Officers' Mess at the barracks on Norfolk Island and was purchased from a furniture maker in Sydney in around 1834.

One of the first significant royal visits to Norfolk Island was in 1946 when Prince Henry, Duke of Gloucester, then serving as the Governor-General of Australia, and Princess Alice, Duchess of Gloucester, were welcomed to the island. They met many of the descendants of the original *Bounty* mutineers, placed a wreath on the First World War memorial and joined a special picnic in their honour, attended by most of the residents of the small island. Queen Elizabeth II visited Norfolk Island in 1974 in a rare royal visit to this remote location when she arrived on the Royal Yacht *Britannia* accompanied by the Duke of Edinburgh, together with Princess Anne and Captain Mark Phillips, en route to Australia. Prince Philip has returned there on more than one occasion.

The picturesque grounds of Government House contain a number of pines and various other trees, while the area around the house is a nature reserve and golf course. A row of the famous Norfolk Island pines was planted adjacent to the main driveway to mark the Silver Jubilee of Queen Elizabeth II in 1977, and in 1988, the visiting Governor-General of Australia, Sir Ninian Stephen, and his wife, Lady Stephen, planted two pines to celebrate the 200th anniversary of Lieutenant Philip Gidley King's arrival in Norfolk Island in 1788.

Below: The colonial-era Government House in Norfolk Island is set in beautiful grounds featuring the famous local pines and a nature reserve.

The grounds are used for official and community functions for Norfolk Island at the discretion of the Administrator, and open days in aid of various charities are held throughout the year. On Bounty Day (8 June), Norfolk Island's national day, Pitcairn descendants' families wearing traditional dress are invited to Government House for a reception following the customary parade. Today, Government House is part of the Kingston and Arthurs Vale Historic Area, a large group of historic buildings from the Australian 'convict' era in the late 18th and early 19th centuries, which is considered to be of such historical and cultural significance that the area is on the Australian National Heritage List and a UNESCO World Heritage Site.

Australia

Government House, The Bahamas

The Bahamas is an archipelago of more than 700 islands in the northern Caribbean and is located south-east of the United States. The Bahamas was the place where explorer Christopher Columbus first landed in the New World in 1492, when the islands were inhabited by the Lucayan, an indigenous people who were later transported to slavery in Hispaniola by the Spanish. The Bahamas were then largely deserted until 1648, when the British landed from Bermuda and The Bahamas became a British Crown Colony in 1718.

This island nation was settled by many American Loyalists following the American War of Independence and the sugar and slave trade that had fuelled the islands' expansion was abolished by the British in 1807; although it wasn't until 1834 that it ceased formally in The Bahamas. Today, The Bahamas is one of the wealthiest countries in the Americas and its capital is Nassau on the island of New Providence.

The Bahamas became an independent Commonwealth realm in 1973, with the monarch represented by a Governor-General. Previously, the Crown was represented by a Governor almost continuously throughout The Bahamas' long history.

The official residence of the Governor-General of The Bahamas is Government House, an impressive coral-pink Georgian building completed in 1806. The house replaced a previous property built in 1737. The steps leading up to the main entrance are dominated by the eye-catching statue of Christopher Columbus, measuring over 3.5 metres (12 feet), which is said to have been designed in London and was made around 1830.

Government House was built on a hill overlooking Nassau, known as Mount Fitzwilliam, and is found on Duke Street. The property is located on a 10-acre (4-hectare) site in the heart of Nassau. The style of the house was said to have been influenced by the Americans from the southern United States who arrived in the islands in the late 18th century, and it is similar

Left: The Duke of Windsor and his wife, the Duchess of Windsor, lived at Government House in Nassau when the Duke was appointed as Governor of The Bahamas in 1940.

Chronicle/Alamy DRHHB4

Above: Government House in The Bahamas is famous for its coral-pink facade and the huge statue of Christopher Columbus that adorns its front steps.

in design to the Parliament of the Bahamas, which is also painted in the distinctive pink colour. The facade of Government House was remodelled in the 1930s following extensive hurricane damage in 1929.

The most famous royal residents of Government House were the Duke and Duchess of Windsor, when the Duke (previously King Edward VIII) was Governor from 1940 to 1945 during the Second World War. They arrived with their two Cairn terriers, Prisie and Pookie. The Duchess of Windsor took up the role of modernising the house and the wide-ranging renovations occured under the supervision of an American architect, Sidney Neil, and an interior decorator, Isabel T. Bradley, who was a socialite friend of the Duchess. A new wing was built for the Windsors', which was later known as the 'Windsor Wing' and is now used by the Royal Bahamas Defence Force as offices. The renovation budget, set at US$6,000 by The Bahamas Government, was well exceeded reaching over US$20,000, however much of the additional cost was paid for by the Duke and Duchess.

It was said that the Duchess wanted to remove the ancient front door at Government House, which had withstood hurricanes and storms over many years, including the famous 1929 hurricane. This proved to be a step too far for the local heritage society who objected, although the Duchess was able to add a glass panel to the door containing the Order of the Garter motto - *Honi soit qui mal y pense* - as a tribute to the Duke who held the honour.

Queen Elizabeth II and Prince Philip visited Government House in The Bahamas when they attended a reception at the start of their Silver Jubilee tour of the Caribbean in October 1977. Many other members of the Royal Family have visited or stayed at Government House over the years. One of the most recent royal visitors to The Bahamas was Prince Harry, when he represented the monarch during the Diamond Jubilee year in 2012.

The Bahamas

Government House, Barbados

Barbados is an island nation in the Caribbean covering just over 160 square miles (415 square kilometres) and is located in the Lesser Antilles group of islands. The indigenous population were the Kalinago people since the 13th century, before the Spanish arrived in the 15th century and claimed the island for the Spanish Crown. However, the Spanish did not remain, and an English ship arrived in Barbados in 1625 to claim the island in the name of King James I.

Barbados was part of the British Empire for many years before becoming an independent Commonwealth realm in 1966. Today, the island has a population of over 280,000 and is a leading tourist destination.

The Crown in Barbados was represented by a Governor from 1627 to 1966 before a Governor-General became the de facto head of state representing the monarch. Government House is the official residence of the Governor-General of Barbados. Located in St Michael, the property was originally a Quaker plantation house known as 'Pilgrim House' which was built in 1702. It was purchased by the government of Barbados and in 1703 was leased as the Governor's formal home.

Previously, Governors of Barbados had lived at the Bagatelle Great House in St Thomas, which was built in 1645 and owned by Scotsman, James Hay, the first Earl of Carlisle, who had been granted permission by King Charles I to colonise the island. The Earl leased the property to the then Governor, Lord Francis Willoughby, who named it, Parnham Park House after his English estate.

Below: Government House was originally a Quaker plantation built in 1702 before it was purchased by the Government of Barbados as an official residence.

Images: Barbados Preservation Heritage Trust

Above: Government House in Barbados has received many royal visitors over the years.

A large, three-storey Georgian residence in Bridgetown, the capital of Barbados, Government House today is the setting for official functions, investitures and receptions hosted by the Governor-General. Garden parties are often held in the grounds, surrounded by tropical flowers, mature mahogany trees and royal palms.

Queen Elizabeth II has visited Barbados several times, notably during her Caribbean Silver Jubilee tour in 1977. A hospital is named in her honour as the Queen Elizabeth Hospital located in Bridgetown. The monarch was represented by the Earl and Countess of Wessex in Barbados during the Diamond Jubilee celebrations at Government House in 2012 and by Prince Harry at Barbados's 50th anniversary of independence celebrations in 2016.

The Prince of Wales and The Duchess of Cornwall also went to the island in 2019, when they called upon the Governor-General of Barbados at Government House and later returned for an evening reception. During a busy schedule in Barbados, the royal couple undertook a wide range of engagements, including a wreath-laying ceremony at the Cenotaph, presenting a new Colour to the Barbados Coast Guard and visiting a local hospital.

Barbados

Government House, Belize

The country of Belize is an independent Commonwealth realm on the eastern coast of Central America, south of Mexico. It has a population of over 380,000 people and covers an area of just under 9,000 square miles (23,000 square kilometres). The early history of Belize was dominated by the Maya civilization, which lived across the Yucatán Peninsula of what is now Mexico, Belize, Guatemala and Honduras. The first Europeans to land in the area were the Spanish in the 16th century, although they chose not to colonize the region of modern-day Belize as Spanish territory. English and Scottish settlers arrived there in the 17th century and began to establish a trade colony to deal in materials including mahogany and clothing dyes.

After long negotiations with the Spanish, a treaty emerged to allow the British to establish the territory of British Honduras in 1862 under the Crown. British Honduras had a chequered history and the economic depression of the 1930s and the collapse of timber values caused much hardship, which was further compounded by a devastating hurricane in 1931, when an estimated 2,500 people lost their lives. Many Belizean men joined the British and Commonwealth armed forces during the Second World War. English is one of the official languages of Belize, while Belizean Creole is also widely spoken.

British Honduras became a self-governing colony in 1964 and was renamed Belize in June 1973, before becoming independent in September 1981. The Crown's representative in Belize was a Superintendent, then Lieutenant-Governor and then a Governor, before the Governor-General assumed the role on independence. Government House in the then capital, Belize City, is said to have been built between 1812 and 1814, at around the same time as the Cathedral of St John the Baptist in Belize, the oldest Anglican Church in Central America.

Below: Government House in the capital, Belize City, is said to have been built between 1812 and 1814.

Right: A collage of images showing the former Government House in Belize and many of the royal and celebrity guests who have visited, including Queen Elizabeth II, Princess Margaret and Princess Mary (also the Princess Royal) during various royal tours of the Caribbean, and Muhammad Ali, the US professional boxer.

The waterfront property was built as the official residence of the Crown and it combined Caribbean colonial and English Georgian architectural styles. The government provided for a cost of no more than £3,000 for its construction, which was a considerable sum at the time. Government House in Belize saw many historic moments in the life of the country. In the 1820s, several Miskito (also known as Mosquito) Kings were crowned at the nearby St John's Cathedral with a reception held at Government House afterwards. In the 1830s, the emancipation of slaves in Belize was observed on the lawns of Government House with a series of special ceremonies.

When the government started construction of the new city of Belmopan in the wake of Hurricane Hattie in 1961, Government House in Belize City was still used as an official residence, although for a time it was almost roofless due to the hurricane damage. On 21 September 1981, the Belize flag was raised for the first time at Government House to mark the newly independent country. The sovereign was represented at the ceremony by Prince Michael of Kent.

In 1998–99, the house became the Belize House of Culture Museum as a way of preserving one of the oldest colonial residences in the country. The museum features exhibitions of glassware, silverware and furniture that were used by successive Governors over many years. It is also used today for government functions, receptions and investitures, and houses the Belize national archives. The former Government House has needed many repairs and been refurbished a number of times. According to the Belize Historical Society, the house has probably been completely rebuilt at least twice.

Since the 1960s, the capital city of Belize had gradually been moved inland to Belmopan. In 1984, the Governor-General's official residence was moved to Belize House in Belmopan, a building that was formerly the residence of the British High Commissioner to Belize.

Queen Elizabeth II first visited Belize in 1985 and again in 1994, although Prince Philip and Princess Margaret had both stayed at Government House prior to this. Since then, Prince Harry is one of the most recent royal visitors to Belize, when he was welcomed on a trip to mark The Queen's Diamond Jubilee in 2012.

Belize

Rideau Hall, Ottawa

Canada is the largest country of the Commonwealth, covering a vast area of nearly 4 million square miles (10 million square kilometres) and stretching from the Atlantic Ocean to the Pacific Ocean. It has one of the longest national land borders, with the United States to the south. Sparsely populated in many areas, many of Canada's 37 million people live in cities today.

The indigenous peoples of Canada lived in the country for many thousands of years before the arrival of European settlers in the 16th and 17th centuries. The French and British established colonies in Canada and there followed a long period of armed conflicts over territory both in Canada and in the United States. By the late 18th century, British North America was a colony controlling much of the eastern region of present-day Canada (including what was then known as Upper and Lower Canada) and the United States.

On 1 July 1867, the colonies of Canada, New Brunswick and Nova Scotia were federated to form the Dominion of Canada. Gradually, many other provinces and territories joined the dominion to form the ten provinces and three territories that make up modern-day Canada. In 1931, the Statute of Westminster recognised Canada's independence from the United Kingdom, but it wasn't until 1982 that Canada finally had its own constitution. The country was also recognised as officially bilingual, with English and French as the national languages at a federal level. Canada is a federal parliamentary democracy with a constitutional monarch as the Canadian head of state, represented by the Governor-General of Canada.

The official residence for the Crown in Canada, in the nation's capital city of Ottawa, is Rideau Hall. The name was derived from the nearby Rideau Falls (the waterfall was said to resemble a curtain or 'rideau') and it remains to this day, although the building is sometimes also referred to as Government House. It was said that Queen Victoria once rebuked one

Above: The original stone villa of Rideau Hall was built in 1838 and was first inhabited by Scottish stonemason, Thomas McKay and his family who were early settlers to Canada.

Vice-Regal Consort, Lady Stanley, for referring to the home as Rideau Hall, as The Queen was of the opinion that all Vice-Regal residences should be known only as Government Houses.

The original stone villa of Rideau Hall was built in around 1838 and was first inhabited by a Scottish stonemason, Thomas McKay, who had bought a large estate for his family outside the settlement of New Edinburgh, which was later to become Ottawa. It was known locally as McKay's Castle.

The residence received many notable visitors at this time, including several Governors-General of Canada and the Prince of Wales (later King Edward VII), who was driven through its grounds on his tour of the region in 1860. By 1864, Rideau Hall, as it was now known, was leased by the Crown from the McKay family as a Vice-Regal residence to replace temporary homes for Governors-General in the area until a formal Government House could be constructed.

The following year, major renovations and additions were undertaken to Rideau Hall, with the construction of a new 49-room, two-storey wing, and the first Governor-General of the new confederation of Canada, Viscount Monck, took up residence. The property was purchased outright by the Crown in 1868 for C$82,000 and Rideau Hall became the centre of the official life of Canadian society. Many of its residents found the furnishings old-fashioned and in need of refurbishment, but despite these initial shortcomings, the house has been in continuous use for successive Governors-General of Canada ever since.

Rideau Hall's first royal residents were John, Marquess of Lorne (later the Duke of Argyll), and his wife, Princess Louise, a daughter of Queen Victoria, who arrived in 1878 when the Marquess took up the post of Governor-General of Canada. As one of the first members of the Royal Family to live in Canada, Princess Louise became a much-loved figure and used her position to support the arts and education. However, she soon became homesick for England and her time in Canada was marred by a bad sleighing accident. The artistic Princess left her mark on the official residence with painted apple branches on a six-panel Georgian door in the first-floor corridor at Rideau Hall, which are similar to those she later painted on the walls and doors at the family seat of Inveraray Castle in Scotland.

In June 1883, the future King George V, then Prince George of Wales, arrived in Canada as a midshipman in the Royal Navy for his first tour of the dominion, and stayed with his aunt and uncle at Rideau Hall.

Right: The apple tree branches on a Georgian door at Rideau Hall were painted by artistic Princess Louise when she lived in the official residence in the 1870s.

Rideau Hall would provide a home to two further 'royal' Governors-General of Canada. Another of Queen Victoria's children, Prince Arthur, Duke of Connaught and Strathearn, was resident from 1911 to 1916 as Governor-General, along with his wife, Princess Louise Margaret, Duchess of Connaught, and their daughter, Princess Patricia of Connaught, who often deputised for her mother at official functions.

One of the biggest additions to Rideau Hall was made in 1913 with the construction of the Mappin Block as a link between the ballroom and other parts of the building. The facade of the block features a relief of the royal coat of arms, said to be one of the largest in the Commonwealth. This addition also included a new porte-cochère (or covered entrance) for formal arrivals.

Canada

Many members of the Royal Family stayed at Rideau Hall on their extensive tours of the dominion in the early 20th century. In 1939, King George VI and Queen Elizabeth spent time there for three days of engagements during the first visit to the country by an incumbent Canadian monarch.

From 1940 to 1946, the uncle of King George VI was appointed as Governor-General of Canada. The Earl of Athlone and his wife, Princess Alice, Countess of Athlone, took up residence at Rideau Hall throughout a key period in Canada's history during the Second World War. The Vice-Regal residence became the home of various displaced and exiled royals from Europe due to the war, many of them related to Princess Alice. They included at different times, Crown Prince Olav (later King Olav V) and Crown Princess Märtha of Norway; Grand Duchess Charlotte and Prince Felix of Luxembourg; King George of the Hellenes; King Peter II of Yugoslavia; Empress Zita of Austria and her daughters; Queen Wilhelmina of the Netherlands, her daughter, Princess Juliana (later Queen Juliana), and her granddaughters, Princesses Beatrix (later Queen Beatrix), Irene and Margriet. Princess Margriet of the Netherlands was born in Ottawa at the Civic Hospital, where the delivery room was temporarily declared as international territory to ensure that the Princess was born as a Dutch national. Princess Alice's own daughter, Lady May Abel Smith, and her three grandchildren, Anne, Richard and Elizabeth also arrived to take refuge from the Second World War in Europe.

The British Prime Minister, Winston Churchill, stayed at Rideau Hall in 1940, from where he continued to direct British wartime activities, and even when a British Government Cabinet meeting took place in London, it was said that he was linked by telephone from his bed at Rideau Hall.

The 1950s saw the appointment of Vincent Massey as the first Canadian-born Governor-General, and Rideau Hall saw many royal and distinguished visitors over the following years which continues today. In 1951, Rideau Hall's first post-war royal visitors were the heiress presumptive to the throne, Princess Elizabeth, Duchess of Edinburgh (later Queen Elizabeth II), and her husband, Philip, Duke of Edinburgh, who engaged in numerous activities, including taking part in a traditional square dance in the Ballroom in their checked shirts. It would be the first of many visits by Queen Elizabeth II to Canada over the years, during which she was often welcomed to Rideau Hall.

Opposite page and right: The formal double-height Ballroom at Rideau Hall was added in the 1870s and it sees many of the formal large-scale ceremonies that take place such as investitures and state banquets.

James Peltzer Photography @james.peltzer

Today, Rideau Hall is the setting for official functions, royal and presidential visits, investitures, diplomatic credentials ceremonies and many other events during the year. The state rooms are open to the public for guided tours throughout the year, welcoming over 200,000 visitors annually. The 175-room residence is located in a quiet suburb of Ottawa on an 88-acre (36-hectare) estate. The main building covers a huge area of 102,000 square feet (9,476 square metres) with several further buildings used for official state and government business.

In 2017, a new Queen's Entrance at Rideau Hall was inaugurated by the Governor-General of Canada, David Johnston, together with the Prince of Wales and the Duchess of Cornwall who were visiting on the occasion of the 150th anniversary of Canada's Confederation. The new forecourt and the wood, glass and bronze doors were created to commemorate the Sapphire Jubilee of Queen Elizabeth II and the 65 years of her reign.

Rideau Hall features many fine furnishings and paintings by prominent Canadian craft-makers and artists, although many Governors-General and their families in the early years brought their own belongings when in residence and so there was a high turnover of contents.

The marble-floored Entrance Hall has a royal window with stained-glass commemorating the 40th anniversary of the accession of Queen Elizabeth II in 1992. The Long Gallery today contains furniture and artefacts that were collected by a Vice-Regal Consort, the Marchioness of Willingdon, throughout her tour of China in 1926.

The formal double-height Ballroom was added at the time of Canada's third Governor-General, the Earl of Dufferin, in the 1870s and it sees many of the formal large-scale ceremonies that take place at Rideau Hall, such as investitures and state banquets. Its powder-blue walls and elaborate ceiling and cornicing were restored in 2005, bringing back the original colours of the room from the period in which it was built.

The Ballroom contains a large Waterford Crystal chandelier weighing over one tonne (1,000 kilogrames) and covered in 12,000 crystals, which was presented by the British government in 1951 in recognition of Canada's central role in the Second World War. The room also features a stained-glass window celebrating Canada's performing arts.

Canada

The Tent Room, with its distinctive red-and-white striped walls and ceiling, is the setting for small receptions and events, although it was originally designed as both an indoor tennis court and a reception room.

Within the Monck Wing, there are further drawing and dining rooms for official use, such as the Pauline Vanier Room, a small sitting room named after the wife of Governor-General, Georges Vanier, where informal meetings are held with visiting heads of state and other officials. The Large Drawing Room, previously the Red Salon, is decorated in the Edwardian style, being renovated in 1901, and the State Dining Room opposite features a large formal table that seats around 42 guests. This part of the residence also contains the formal Governor-General's Study, overlooking the gardens and dating from 1906, with a smaller office for the Vice-Regal Consort next door. The Canadian Prime Minister and important guests are received in the study, which is lined with carved wood panels noting the names of successive incumbents around the room.

Rideau Hall features many further formal rooms and guest suites for both the Vice-Regal couple and visiting dignitaries, as well as a small chapel for both Anglican and Catholic services, which was formally consecrated in 1967 in the presence of Queen Elizabeth II.

Many paintings are on permanent loan from the National Gallery of Canada or form part of the Crown Collection for Government House. The house has prominent paintings of numerous monarchs on display including Queen Victoria, Queen Elizabeth II and various famous Canadians. Rideau Hall was designated as a National Historic Site of Canada in 1977 and many restoration projects have been undertaken, including a restoration of the building's main facade in 2006–07.

Above and left: The Tent Room, with its unique red-and-white striped walls and ceiling, is one of the most recognisable rooms at Rideau Hall.

James Peltzer Photography @james.peltzer

The grounds of Rideau Hall contain wide lawns, formal gardens, and a greenhouse and flower gardens that provide produce for the main residence. There are numerous trees planted by royal and formal visitors, and there are also indigenous sculptures, a totem pole and the inukshuk representing the many different peoples of Canada. The Fountain of Hope marks the International Year of Disabled Persons and the Canadian Heritage Garden is a formal rose garden created to mark the 125th anniversary of Canada's Confederation.

Throughout its history as a royal park, the gardens at Rideau Hall have hosted numerous activities often connected to the winter weather, providing rinks for ice skating and curling and also toboggan runs. Garden parties are held in the summer months and the cricket pitch that is still in use today was first laid out in 1866 under Viscount Monck. Concerns over security and terrorism reduced the public's access to the grounds for some years but this has been reversed in recent times. Rideau Hall is also one of the few places in the Commonwealth outside of Buckingham Palace and Windsor Castle that has military sentries outside and a formal changing of the guard ceremony.

Rideau Hall's grounds also contain many other buildings used by the Office of the Governor-General, the Royal Canadian Mounted Police and Government Services Canada, as well as Rideau Cottage, a 22-room house built in 1867 as a residence for the Governor-General's official secretary, which has recently been used as a family home by the Canadian Prime Minister.

Two further notable buildings connected to Rideau Hall are also located nearby. St Bartholomew's Anglican Church, built in the late 19th century, is used regularly as a place of worship by Governors-General and visiting members of the Royal Family. The church contains a beautiful stained-glass window by young Irish artist, Wilhelmina Geddes, that was commissioned by Prince Arthur, Duke of Connaught, shortly after the First World War and is dedicated to the memory of the members of his household killed in the war. In addition, 7 Rideau Gate is a large property opposite the forecourt of the main gate to Rideau Hall that is often used as an official guesthouse for visitors to Canada.

As the main official residence for the Governors-General of Canada, Rideau Hall has seen many events and ceremonies in the formal life of the country and has played host to royalty, presidents and prime ministers over the years.

Canada

La Citadelle, Québec City

The Governor-General of Canada has a second official residence located at La Citadelle in Québec in recognition of the importance of the French-speaking areas of the country and their place in Canadian national life. The city of Québec was founded in 1608 by Samuel de Champlain.

Essentially a military fortress, La Citadelle was constructed between 1820 and 1832 in Québec City, although some parts of the fortress date back further such as the ramparts and the Cap-aux-Diamants redoubt (the fort's square parade ground) dating from 1693. The fortress played a key role in the many battles of the North American colonies between the French, the British and the newly formed military of Canada and the United States.

La Citadelle is one of the oldest military buildings in Canada and forms part of the fortifications of Québec City, which is today a National Historic Site of Canada and a UNESCO World Heritage Site, receiving around 200,000 visitors each year. From the air, the citadel forms an uneven star-shape, with around 24 buildings within its thick walls.

The formal home of the Governor-General at La Citadelle is found in part of the former garrison buildings, which were first constructed in around 1831 in the neoclassical style. It was originally occupied by British officers until their departure in 1871, when the Earl of Dufferin became the first Governor-General of Canada to take up residence in La Citadelle in 1872. Most Governors-General since then have spent time there while undertaking official duties.

Further additions to the building were made over the years, including a ballroom and sunroom overlooking the St Lawrence River. Unfortunately, a major fire in February 1976 completely destroyed these additions – although the building's west wing was restored. New state rooms were opened in 1984 featuring a mix of military and modern styles of Canada, with furniture described as being in the New-France style.

La Citadelle is a large residence comprising over 100 rooms, and its visitors enter through a classical porch which features the words 'Gouverneur Général' and a heraldic lion.

Since 1920, La Citadelle has been the home barracks for the Royal 22e Régiment of the Canadian Forces and it remains a military base today. Built in 1750, Building 15, or the powder magazine, is the home of the Museum of the Royal 22e Régiment and the Canadian Forces Museum, displaying many Canadian military artefacts.

During the Second World War, La Citadelle played a key role as the venue for the 1943 and 1944 Québec Conferences, where the Governor-General of Canada, then the Earl of Athlone, hosted the Prime Minister of Canada, William Mackenzie-King, the British Prime Minister, Winston Churchill and the President of the United States, Franklin D. Roosevelt to discuss their war strategies.

Below: La Citadelle is one of the few places other than Buckingham Palace and Windsor Castle to hold regular military changing of the guard ceremonies.

Today, La Citadelle accommodates the Governor-General for several weeks during the summer and at other times of the year when official receptions, investitures and presentations are held. The residence has an extensive education programme for local schools and is open to the public throughout the year. Military changing of the guard ceremonies take place in the summer months similar to those held at Rideau Hall, Buckingham Palace and Windsor Castle.

Meunierd/Shutterstock 1133894918

Canada

Spencerwood, Québec

Alamy MM3M18

Left: Spencerwood was the official residence of the Lieutenant-Governor of Québec between 1870 and 1966, when it was destroyed by fire. Considered to be Québec's Government House, it is pictured circa 1910.

In Canada, the province of Québec is predominantly French-speaking. One of the largest geographic areas of Canada, it also has the second-largest population of nearly 9 million people. Québec has a long and somewhat complex history. The indigenous peoples of the region were the Algonquian, Iroquois, Inuit and later the Mohawk nation. The French began to explore the area in the mid-1500s and early settlements were established in what became known as New France. In 1603, Samuel de Champlain arrived from France to explore the area around the St Lawrence River and he returned in 1608 to establish the city of Québec.

New France fought off several attempts by the British to take over the settlement, but in 1759, the British defeated the French at the Plains of Abraham outside Québec City and New France became part of the British colonies under the terms of the Treaty of Paris in 1763. The creation of Upper Canada (Ontario) and Lower Canada (Québec) in 1791 allowed the British settlers in Upper Canada to live under British laws and institutions, while the French-speaking population of Lower Canada was able to maintain French civil law and the Catholic religion. The Canadian monarch was represented in Lower Canada (later known as Canada East before it became Québec) by a series of Governors and then the Lieutenant-Governor of Québec, a role which has been in existence since 1867 when Québec joined the Confederation of Canada.

Built in 1854, Spencerwood was located in the Bois-de-Coulonge Park and was purchased by the Québec Government in 1870 as an official residence for the Lieutenant-Governor. It was an impressively large house with Palladian-style columns adorning the front and comfortable formal reception rooms inside. Royal visitors to Spencerwood during its time as Government House for Québec included the Duke and Duchess of Cornwall and York (later King George V and Queen Mary) in 1901, King George VI and Queen Elizabeth in 1939, and Queen Elizabeth II and Prince Philip in 1964.

However, there has been no established Vice-Regal residence in Québec since 1997, when a former official home, known as Dunn's House, was sold by the provincial government. Lieutenant-Governors resided at Dunn's House from 1967 to 1997. This was as a result of the former residence of Spencerwood, considered to be Québec's Government House, being devastated by a fire in 1966. Sadly, the Lieutenant-Governor at the time, Paul Comtois, died in the blaze which destroyed the house.

Today, the Lieutenant-Governor of Québec has an official office suite at 1050, rue des Parlementaires in Québec City, a Beaux-Arts building owned by the Government of Québec. Formal ceremonies, the swearing-in of Ministers and the receiving of VIP guests to the province all take place at the suite.

Government House, Alberta

Alberta is a western landlocked region of Canada, the most populated of Canada's three Prairie Provinces. It was established as a Canadian province in 1905 and its capital city is Edmonton.

It is said that Alberta was named after Princess Louise Caroline Alberta, the fourth daughter of Queen Victoria, who was the Vice-Regal Consort to Canada when her husband, John Campbell, Marquess of Lorne, was the Governor-General of Canada between 1878 and 1883. Notable tourist destinations in Alberta, such as the famous Lake Louise and Mount Alberta were also said to have been named after the Princess.

In common with the other Canadian provinces, the Canadian monarch is represented by a Lieutenant-Governor in Alberta, who undertakes a similar ceremonial role as the Governor-General but at a provincial level. Government House, Alberta is the main ceremonial property, although technically this house is no longer an official residence as the Lieutenant-Governor today lives elsewhere.

Alberta's Government House is located in the Glenora suburb of Edmonton. The house has been extensively restored and is currently used by the provincial government of Alberta for ceremonial events and conferences, although it no longer offers accommodation.

The property and the 28-acre (11-hectare) estate were first purchased by the province of Alberta in 1910 and construction began on a new residence for the Lieutenant-Governor in 1912, before finally opening in October 1913. The three-storey structure was built in local sandstone in the Jacobean Revival style, with stonemasons coming from Scotland to complete its construction. Unique at the time for a Government House was the installation of a passenger lift to the upper floors, which was entered just off the main hallway.

Royal visitors to the residence were rare, but the Prince of Wales (later Edward VIII) stayed at Government House in Edmonton for the first time in 1919 on one of his extensive overseas tours and he would return to the house several times over the years after he acquired a ranch in High River, Alberta.

Canada

Government House was used as a Vice-Regal home for six successive Lieutenant-Governors until 1938, when the Alberta government closed the building citing economic problems. A political row arose when the Lieutenant-Governor of Alberta, John C. Bowen, refused to give royal assent to three controversial Bills in the Legislative Assembly and so the subsequent closure of Government House was seen as an act of retaliation by the then Alberta Premier, William Aberhart.

Sadly, the building and its furniture were sold and the property was used as a boarding house for American pilots who were supplying the construction of the Alaska Highway. Later, it became a military hospital during the Second World War and then a home for veterans afterwards. In 1964, the house and grounds were returned to the provincial Crown.

The main residence was restored in the mid-1970s at a cost of C$1.7 million and has hosted many important functions in the life of the province, including visits by Queen Elizabeth II and Prince Philip during the Commonwealth Games, which were held in Edmonton in 1978, the Prince and Princess of Wales on their tour in 1983 and Pope John Paul II in 1984.

The Queen and the Duke of Edinburgh returned to Government House in 2005, when they attended events as part of Alberta's centennial celebrations. More recently in 2018, the Princess Royal visited Government House in Alberta for an official engagement to unveil the first marker of the Edmonton Commonwealth Walkway, which explores both Edmonton's history and Canada's Commonwealth heritage.

Today, both the Lieutenant-Governor of Alberta and the Alberta Government use the reception rooms at Government House and the conference centre for official functions. For example, the Lieutenant-Governor presides over the swearing-in ceremonies for new Cabinet Ministers that take place at Government House following an election, while the

Below: Built in 1912–13, Government House in Alberta is no longer an official residence of the Lieutenant-Governor, but is today used for official events and ceremonies.

Image: Courtesy of the Office of the Lieutenant-Governor of Alberta

Above: The suite of official rooms used by the Lieutenant-Governor in the Alberta Legislative Buildings in downtown Edmonton has been in use since 1912 and continues to be used today.

caucus of the main governing party meets in the Alberta Room, a 100-seat conference room on the top floor of the house. When not in use for official business, the former residence is open to the public and many original pieces of furniture have been returned to the property.

In 2005, Gangwon Province in South Korea constructed a traditional Korean Jeongja or pavilion named 'Gangwonjeong' in the grounds of Government House in Edmonton as a centennial gift to the province of Alberta and also to celebrate the 30th anniversary of the twinning relationship between the two provinces.

Separate to Government House, the Lieutenant-Governor of Alberta has the use of a suite of official rooms and an office at the Legislative Buildings of Alberta in downtown Edmonton. These formal rooms have been used by the Lieutenant-Governor since 1912 and continue to be used today. Official visitors to the province are received in the suite and small receptions are also held there. The suite features original furniture from the Legislature along with the province's official guest book, signed by Queen Elizabeth II and many members of the Royal Family, all of the Governors-General of Canada since 1935 and other important visitors to Alberta.

Canada

Government House, British Columbia

British Columbia is the most westerly province of Canada on the Pacific Ocean coast. The first British settlement was established at Fort Victoria in 1843, which was initially the capital of the separate colony of Vancouver Island before it joined with the mainland colony of British Columbia. First Nations people, the original inhabitants of the land, have a history of at least 10,000 years in the area.

Richard Clement Moody, who founded British Columbia, became the first Lieutenant-Governor and set about transforming the region into the most prosperous outpost of the British Empire. Moody selected New Westminster as the first capital of British Columbia, but this was later moved to Victoria on Vancouver Island when the two colonies merged. In 1871, British Columbia became the sixth province of Canada.

Government House in Victoria is the official residence of the Lieutenant-Governor of British Columbia, although as it is situated in a quiet suburb of the city, the house has the feel of a large suburban home. Set in a 36-acre (14.5-hectare) estate at 1401 Rockland Avenue, it is not the original Government House for the province on this site.

The first residence of the Lieutenant-Governor was Cary Castle, a stone villa built in 1859 by George Cary as a Victorian mock-Tudor castle and purchased six years later by the provincial Crown as a Vice-Regal home for the Governor of Vancouver. Following the merger of Vancouver Island and British Columbia as one province, and the establishment of Victoria as the capital, Cary Castle maintained its place as the official abode of the Crown.

Although the province was remote, as the Canadian-Pacific railway had yet to be constructed, Government House at Cary Castle did eventually receive its first royal visit from the Canadian Governor-General, John, Marquess of Lorne, and his wife, Princess Louise, in 1882. Their arrival generated much interest in this isolated part of Canada and there was a carnival atmosphere in Victoria. The Princess sketched the house and its scenic views of forests and mountains, and found that the location reminded her of the Balmoral Estate in Scotland.

Unfortunately, Cary Castle was destroyed by fire in May 1899, although a replacement was immediately commissioned to designs by architects Francis Rattenbury and Samuel Maclure, and was completed by 1903. This left a rather awkward situation when the Duke and Duchess of Cornwall and York (later King George V and Queen Mary) came to British

Below: The main entrance to Government House in British Columbia features the original Tudor-style porte cochère of a previous Government House.

Cameron Knowlton

Above: The gardens at Government House are often open to the public, and used by the local community.

Colombia in 1901, on their far-reaching global tour of the British Empire. However, the royal couple and their entourage stayed at the Mount Baker Hotel in Oak Bay, while the state dinner to mark their visit was held at the Lieutenant-Governor's temporary residence named Gyppeswyk in Mount Street.

The second Government House was visited for the first time by a reigning monarch when King George VI and Queen Elizabeth arrived in 1939 as part of their extensive tour across Canada. Princess Elizabeth stayed at the house in 1951 when, as Duchess of Edinburgh, she toured the province with Prince Philip. British Prime Minister, Winston Churchill and United States President, Franklin D. Roosevelt also stayed at the house during this period.

Sadly, history was repeated when the second Government House caught fire in April 1957 and most of the residence was again ruined. The current and third Government House on this site was completed in May 1959 by John Laing and Sons. The incumbent Lieutenant-Governor of British Columbia, Frank Mackenzie Ross, helped to furnish the new property with items bought in the United Kingdom, before he donated them to the Crown along with furniture from many British Columbian craftspeople.

The present-day Government House is a T-shaped, four-storey residence in a mock-Tudor-style with blue, grey and pink British Columbia granite exterior walls. The roof features chalet-like gables and dormer windows, giving the house a unique appearance. The original Tudor-style porte cochère of the previous Government House survives above the main entrance, which leads to the entrance hall lined with portraits of Queen Elizabeth II and Prince Philip, and previous Lieutenant-Governors of British Columbia. The room is dominated by the Rogers Window, a stained-glass window unveiled in 1990 and commissioned by Vice-Regal Consort, Jane Rogers, to commemorate British Columbia's heritage.

The largest room in the house is the Ballroom, which occupies the whole south wing and rises to a height of 12 metres with three Swiss-cut crystal chandeliers. A vast, south-facing

Canada

bow window at one end of the Ballroom gives commanding views of the Ross Bay and beyond, as far as the mountains of Washington state in the United States. The Ballroom also features the stained-glass Millennium Windows, which were designed in 2000 to commemorate the natural beauty and landscapes of British Columbia.

The fir-wood-panelled State Dining Room features a dining suite purchased in Scotland, that can seat up to 40 people. The small drawing room is sometimes called the French Drawing Room because it has many decorative objects of French origin, including a Sèvres clock and numerous porcelain vases.

The Maclure Room is found on the lower-ground floor of Government House and is named after Samuel Maclure, one of the architects of the previous Government House. The room is decorated in the Arts and Crafts-style with furniture from the late 19th and early 20th century. The Rattenbury Room, also named after an architect involved with the 1903 residence, is the Lieutenant-Governor's personal dining room and is used for intimate dining with ambassadors and other guests. Government House features many artworks from the Crown collection, including artworks by British Columbia First Nations artists.

Government House today hosts over 150 ceremonial events each year, including investitures to the Order of British Columbia and the popular Lieutenant-Governors' New Year's levées, where members of public have the opportunity to visit the residence.

Covering over 36-acres (14-hectares), the gardens at Government House are often open to the public, and used by the local community. The grounds feature many different gardens, such as one containing native British Columbia plant life and another rose garden that is originally based on a design for Warwick Castle in England. Conservation and sustainability are key features of the gardens and they provide a unique ecosystem for wildlife and insects.

In 2002, Government House and its surrounding gardens were designated as a National Historic Site of Canada. As with other Government Houses in Canada, the residence in British Columbia is owned by the provincial Crown, though the management of the house is overseen by the British Columbia Government House Foundation, a charitable, non-profit organisation that was established in 1987.

Many members of the Royal Family have visited Government House in British Columbia several times, including recent visits by Queen Elizabeth II and Prince Philip, the Prince of Wales and the Duchess of Cornwall, the Earl and Countess of Wessex and the Duke of York, as well as the Emperor and Empress of Japan and Queen Noor of Jordan.

Most recently in 2016, the Duke and Duchess of Cambridge were welcomed with their young children, Prince George and Princess Charlotte, who attended a special children's tea party for military families held in the gardens of Government House.

Above: The wood-panelled State Dining Room at Government House is used for formal dinners.

Below: The formal rooms at Government House feature royal portraits, artworks and fine furniture.

Government House, Manitoba

Manitoba is the most easterly of the three Canadian Prairie Provinces and is found in the centre of Canada. It is sparsely populated, considering its size, and it borders the United States in the south.

Indigenous peoples lived in the area for many thousands of years until European fur traders arrived in the late 17th century, when it became part of Rupert's Land controlled by the Hudson Bay Company. When negotiations for the creation of the province began in 1869, an armed conflict known as the Red River Rebellion started with the Métis people, but the government prevailed and Manitoba was recognised as a province of Canada in 1870. The capital city was established in the largest settlement of Winnipeg.

Government House, the historic residence of the Lieutenant-Governor of Manitoba, is found at 10 Kennedy Street, on the grounds of the Manitoba Legislative Building, in downtown Winnipeg. This gives the residence a unique location at the heart of the province's political and urban life.

Below: Government House in Winnipeg is a three-storey residence that was built in 1883.

The three-storey residence was built at the request of the Dominion Canadian Government in 1883 at a cost of C$24,000. An initial design was drawn up by Dominion Architect, Thomas Seaton Scott, and it was this design that provided the outline structure for Government House.

Terrance Klassen/Alamy B3X9J6

Canada

It was described by the provincial architects as *"Victorian architecture with a French influence from the Second Napoleonic Empire with the flat steep-sided Mansard roof."*[1]

The flag tower gives the house the stately feel of a small French-style chateau and the Lieutenant-Governor's standard is flown from the mast when he or she is in residence.

In 1885, the ownership of the property was transferred from the Dominion Government of Canada to the Provincial Government of Manitoba for the princely sum of C$1 with the stipulation that it was always to be used as an official Vice-Regal residence.

The words 'and for no other purpose' were written by the first Prime Minister of Canada, Sir John A. Macdonald, in his own hand on the margin of the Order-in-Council (official documents) for the transfer of the property.

The present Government House replaced an earlier temporary residence located inside the walls of Upper Fort Garry in Hudson's Bay, which was occupied by the first Lieutenant-Governor of Manitoba, Adams Archibald. The Lieutenant-Governor chose the temporary house as the first Government House in early 1870, which was a former home of the last Governor of Rupert's Land. It was owned by the Hudson's Bay Company and Archibald remained there until 1883, when the current building at 10 Kennedy Street was completed.

Today, Government House has 23 rooms and 11 bathrooms covering over 20,000 square feet (1,850 square metres) in size, but there have been many changes made over the years. The interior has elegant decor but some of the original 19th century features haven't survived. For example, only two of the six plaster ceiling rosettes remain in the house in the entrance hall and in the Manitoba Room.

Above and below: Government House in Manitoba features many historical and royal artefacts.

[1]Reference: Manitoba Government House website www.manitobalg.ca

Garry Robinson

Garry Robinson

The Aides Room, also known as the Manitoba Room, is a small room inside the front entrance where guests sign the visitors' book. A State Ballroom was added in 1901 for the visit of the Duke and Duchess of Cornwall and York (later King George V and Queen Mary) to Manitoba – however, this was later demolished and the present Ballroom (or Assembly Room) was built in 1960.

The State Dining Room, known originally as the Palm Room, was added in 1908. A kitchen wing was constructed in 1946, replacing the original basement kitchen.

The furniture in the house dates mainly from the late Victorian period, although modern pieces have been added over the years. One of the residence's prized possessions is a table in the Library dating from around 1900. A small brass plaque commemorates the 'Winnipeg' speech made by King George VI to the Empire at the table on 24 May 1939 while broadcasting from Government House on Empire Day, now Victoria Day. King George VI and Queen Elizabeth stayed in Manitoba during their historic 1939 tour of Canada and the United States. Queen Elizabeth II and Prince Philip have visited Government House in Manitoba a number of times, with the first occasion in 1951 and most recently in 2010.

The grounds of Government House, featuring formal gardens, run around three sides of the residence. One section was named the Queen Elizabeth II Gardens by The Queen during her 2010 visit, when a special tree was planted and a 1970 statue of the monarch that had originally been outside the Manitoba Centennial Centre was moved to the newly dedicated gardens.

Above and below: The furniture at Government House is a mixture of original and donated.

The residence is the official home of the Lieutenant-Governor and hosts a wide range of functions, receptions and events throughout the year. Government House in Manitoba has an important place in the province's heritage and remains a significant local landmark.

Canada

Government House, New Brunswick

New Brunswick is one of Canada's three Maritime Provinces on the Atlantic east coast. The Mi'kmaq, the Maliseet and the Passamaquoddy were the indigenous peoples of the area and the French arrived in the early 1600s. New Brunswick became part of Nova Scotia in 1755, before separating as a distinct province in 1784. In 1867, New Brunswick was one of four founding provinces of Canada, along with Nova Scotia, Québec and Ontario.

The provincial capital was moved from the first settlement of St John to St Anne's Point further inland and, in 1785, King's College (now the University of New Brunswick) became one of the first universities in North America. The small capital grew and was renamed 'Frederick's Town' in honour of the second son of King George III, Prince Frederick Augustus, Duke of York – although the name was later shortened to Fredericton.

Government House in Fredericton is the official residence of the Lieutenant-Governor of New Brunswick. The house is located at 51 Woodstock Road along the St John River from the capital. The grounds cover an estate of around 11-acres (4.5-hectares) and the site was once a 17th century Acadian settlement known as Sainte-Anne.

The large Georgian-style sandstone building was built between 1826 and 1828 to replace an earlier wooden house that burned down in 1825. The sandstone was quarried locally in New Brunswick and Government House is one of the oldest houses in the area made from local stone. The property was designed by English architect James Woolford as an elegant Vice-Regal residence, featuring a curved portico and shallow roof gable with its small rose window. Woolford also designed several other local buildings, including Fredericton Barracks and the Old Arts Building at the University of New Brunswick.

The layout of Government House has changed little since it was built, with a large drawing room, dining room and music room on the ground floor for official functions as well as the Lieutenant-Governor's original office. The second floor has exhibition rooms and modern

Diane Lanteigne

Diane Lanteigne

Above and opposite page: The large Georgian-style Government House in New Brunswick was built between 1826 and 1828.

offices for the Lieutenant-Governor and their staff, while the third floor has a private Vice-Regal apartment.

For many years, Government House hosted meetings of the Executive Council, as well as Vice-Regal dinners and balls for the high society of the province. Royalty even came to stay, requiring preparations to be made and new furniture ordered. The Prince of Wales (later King Edward VII) visited Fredericton in 1860, when he inaugurated a new park and fountain in the capital. After his departure, however, the provincial government were said to have auctioned off the extra furnishings purchased for the house, which was perhaps a prelude to what was to come in later years. Queen Victoria's second son, Prince Alfred, Duke of Edinburgh, came to stay in 1869, to be followed by the Canadian Governor-General, the Marquess of Lorne, and his wife, Princess Louise, in 1879.

However, in 1890, the Lieutenant-Governor of New Brunswick, Samuel Leonard Tilley, considered the cost of running Government House to be too high and he moved out. There followed a 109-year period with no Vice-Regal residents in the property and Lieutenant-Governors in New Brunswick rented other places in the area, including Somerville House, an 1820s house that was also reputed to have been designed by the same architect as Government House, James Woolford. The lack of an official residence did affect many plans for royal visits to the area, as there wasn't a suitable venue to host the royal guests.

From 1896 to 1900, Government House served as the New Brunswick Institute for the Deaf, followed by a time as a military barracks during the First World War. Between 1934 and 1988, the house was the regional headquarters for the Royal Canadian Mounted Police. In 1959, a garden party was held in the grounds of Government House, when Queen Elizabeth II and Prince Philip visited New Brunswick on one of several visits to the province.

Canada

The heritage value of the house was recognised in 1958 when it was designated as a National Historic Site of Canada, but it wasn't until 1999, after two years of extensive renovations by local craftspeople, that Government House was returned to its original purpose as a Vice-Regal residence.

The renovations, at a cost of C$5.5 million, were supported by the Canadian Federal Government, the New Brunswick Provincial Government and Fredericton City Council, and were considered a 'once in a lifetime' project to return Government House to its original grandeur and to share the house with the public. An 1835 painting

titled 'Indian Dance', depicting a New Year's levée at Government House, was used by the restoration team to match the decor, furnishings and carpets as close as possible to the original designs.

A number of historic furniture items in Government House today are pieces that had belonged to the original house from the early 1800s, including a dining-room table, chairs and sofas, and three chandeliers. According to historical records, around 400 pieces of furniture from the Government House collection were auctioned in 1897, however, since its reopening in 1999, around 150 pieces have been donated, returned or purchased for the property. Today, Government House is the place where royal and distinguished visitors to the province are entertained, appointments to the Order of New Brunswick are made and official functions are held. The residence is often open to the public, who can take the opportunity to share in the story of this historic building.

All images: Diane Lanteigne

Left and above: Much of the furnishings at Government House today have been donated, returned or purchased for the property, following a 109-year period when the building was used by numerous different organisations.

Garry Robinson

Government House, Newfoundland and Labrador

As the most easterly province of Canada on the Atlantic Ocean coastline, Newfoundland and Labrador is made up of the island of Newfoundland and the mainland region of Labrador. With a population of just over 500,000 people and an area of over 150,000 square miles (388,000 square kilometres), the area is sparsely populated with 40% of people living in the province's capital, St John's.

Many European settlers arrived in the area, but it was the English, under Sir Humphrey Gilbert, who claimed the land as a colony in the name of Queen Elizabeth I in 1583. British sovereignty was recognised by the Treaty of Utrecht in 1713 and there followed several further treaties with the French over the disputed territory before Newfoundland became a dominion of the British Empire in 1907.

Newfoundland faced economic difficulties following the First World War and the Great Depression, and the province relinquished its independence in 1933 to be administered by Commissioners, before joining the Confederation in 1949 as the tenth province of Canada. In 2001, the province changed its official name to Newfoundland and Labrador.

The monarch is represented in the province by the Lieutenant-Governor (previously the Governor) of Newfoundland and Labrador. The first Governors were naval officers who were stationed on their flagship, usually anchored in St John's harbour, throughout the summers. The harsh winters in Canada meant that the official administration often went back to England to avoid the severe cold.

Admiral Richard Edwards decided that the Governor should live ashore and engaged Royal Artillery Lieutenant, John Thomas Caddy, to design a house within the newly completed Fort Townshend in St John's. The building was completed in 1781 and was a two-storey property that formed one side of the barrack's square. Governors were gradually persuaded to spend the winters in Newfoundland, although the unfortunate Sir Francis Pickmore reported that snow came into the bedrooms of the house during a severe storm in the winter of 1817–18 and he later died from pneumonia.

Canada

The construction of a new Government House got underway in 1827 to a plan drawn up in England, with 28 masons, 25 carpenters and a slater brought over from Scotland to work on the house. The building work was overseen by the British Army regiment, the Royal Engineers, who were stationed nearby in Newfoundland.

The large two-storey house was completed in 1831 using local red sandstone trimmed with English Portland stone, but the project had run severely over budget with costs increasing to an estimated £38,000, five times the original estimate and a huge sum at the time. The first Governor to live in Government House was Sir Thomas Cochrane and his family.

The interior was designed with spacious, elegant formal rooms in the Regency-style. The main entrance hall opens up to a decorative oval balustrade on the first floor and a cupola (dome) in the roof of the house. The principal rooms include a large salon, dining room and ballroom, which remain largely unchanged today.

The furniture in Government House has also survived intact since 1831. The Spanish mahogany dining-room table dates from the period and can seat 24 people for formal lunches and dinners when all seven additional leaves are added. Georgian mahogany sideboards and zinc-lined wooden wine chests complete the set.

A mahogany canopy bed, which features a wood-carving of the Prince of Wales's feathers, was made in 1860 for the visit of the Prince of Wales (later King Edward VII) to Newfoundland.

Government House in St John's has welcomed many royal guests, including King George V and Queen Mary when they were the Duke and Duchess of Cornwall and York during

Above: Government House in Newfoundland and Labrador was constructed from local red sandstone and imported English Portland stone and it was completed in 1831.

their tour of Canada in 1901; Prince Arthur, Duke of Connaught, in 1914 when he was Governor-General of Canada; the Prince of Wales (later King Edward VIII) in 1919; and King George VI and Queen Elizabeth on their 1939 tour of the country.

Queen Elizabeth II paid her first visit to Government House in Newfoundland with Prince Philip in 1959 as part of their Canada-wide tour. The Queen returned in 1978 when she went to the site of what would become the Queen Elizabeth II Library at the Memorial University of Newfoundland. Two twin mahogany canopy beds in a Hepplewhite-style that were made by Ralph Clements for the royal visit that year can still be seen at Government House.

The Queen also returned in 1997, when she was present for the celebrations for the 500th anniversary of the landfall of explorer John Cabot in Newfoundland, when a replica of Cabot's ship, *The Matthew*, sailed into the harbour. The most recent royal visitors to Government House were the Prince of Wales and the Duchess of Cornwall in 2009.

Above right: Visitors to Government House enter through the lobby into the main entrance hall.

Government House in Newfoundland and Labrador was designated as a National Historic Site of Canada in 1982 and today is the official residence of the Lieutenant-Governor.

Canada

Scott Baltjes

Government House, Nova Scotia

Nova Scotia is one of the three Maritime Provinces of Canada on the Atlantic coast and its name derives from the Latin for 'New Scotland', following its settlement by Scottish traders. The second smallest of Canada's provinces at 21,000 square metres, it includes over 3,500 small islands. The province was inhabited by the Mi'kmaq nation before the first European settlers arrived from France in 1605 to establish the region of Acadia with its main town of Port-Royal. However, in 1710 the British conquest of Acadia took place and the Treaty of Utrecht in 1713 formally recognised Nova Scotia as a British settlement. Port-Royal was renamed Annapolis Royal in honour of Queen Anne, although in 1749 the provincial capital moved to the new city of Halifax.

Nova Scotia became one of the four founding provinces of the Canadian Confederation in 1867 and it was at this time that the modern position of Lieutenant-Governor of Nova Scotia was established to represent the monarch, replacing earlier Governors in the area.

The construction of the official residence of Government House is largely credited to one of the earlier Governors of Nova Scotia, Sir John Wentworth, who arrived in Halifax in 1792. He objected to the poor conditions and 'green wood and rotting timbers' of the old Governor's home. Wentworth noted that some of the land purchased by the government for a new Legislative Assembly building was surplus to requirements and it was considered at the time to be too far from the centre of the capital for the Legislature, so he set about commissioning a suitable official residence on the land instead.

Government House in Nova Scotia was built between 1799 and 1805, making it one of the oldest continuously occupied official residences in North America. The house was modelled on a Georgian English country residence of the time, with symmetrical windows

Scott Bathjes

Right: The most significant painting in the house is the portrait of the Governor of Nova Scotia, Sir John Wentworth, by Robert Field dating from around c.1808.

and chimneys and matching bow wings in the style of the English architect, Robert Adam. The architect for Government Houses House was Isaac Hildreth, a Yorkshireman who had emigrated to Virginia in the United States of America in 1770, where he had furthered his reputation following several successful building projects.

Local stone, sand and wood was used in the construction of the house with additional mahogany from South America for the doors and panelling, Scottish slate for the roof and marble fireplace mantles fashioned in London. The house has been refurbished several times in its history, but many original features remain. The interior was arranged for formal events and receptions with a large drawing room, dining room and ballroom, as well as rooms for the Lieutenant-Governor and their family. The most significant painting in the house is the portrait of the man responsible for the property, the Governor, Sir John Wentworth, by Robert Field, painted in around c.1808.

Halifax was an important and strategic port in the north Atlantic Ocean, and as a result many royal visitors came to stay. Prince Edward, Duke of Kent, the father of Queen Victoria, was appointed the Commander of the British forces in Nova Scotia in 1794 and he stayed in Halifax with his mistress, Julie de Saint-Laurent, until the end of the 18th century, just prior to the construction of the present Government House.

The first royal visitor to stay at Government House in Nova Scotia was the Prince of Wales (later King Edward VII) in 1860. It was a great event in the province and the drawing room and dining room were refurbished for the visit, with the Prince of Wales's feathers added to the window cornices. Three more of Queen Victoria's children came to stay there in subsequent years: Prince Arthur, Duke of Connaught, visited in 1869 and he enjoyed a moose hunt among many other country pursuits; while Princess Louise arrived in 1878 with her husband, the Marquess of Lorne, then the Governor-General of Canada, to be met by her brother, Prince Alfred, Duke of Edinburgh, who was the Commanding Officer of one of the Royal Navy's ships stationed in Halifax at the time.

Image: Courtesy of Government House, Nova Scotia

Right: Government House in Nova Scotia was built between 1799 and 1805, making it one of the oldest continuously occupied official residences in North America.

Canada

Prince George of Wales (later King George V) visited Government House when he was serving with the North Atlantic Fleet in 1883–84, and he would return in 1901 as the Duke of Cornwall and York with his wife, Princess Mary, Duchess of Cornwall and York (later Queen Mary), on their extensive tour of the British Empire. Two of their sons were later welcomed to Nova Scotia: Prince Albert (later King George VI) as a naval cadet in 1913 and the Prince of Wales (later King Edward VIII) on

Image: Courtesy of Government House, Nova Scotia

Left and below left: Government House in Nova Scotia has been refurbished several times in its long history, but many original features remain in the grand entrance hall and the ballroom.

his first Canadian tour in 1919. King George VI would return in 1939 as the first Canadian monarch to stay at Government House in Halifax with Queen Elizabeth. In recognition of the province's connections to her Scottish birthplace, Queen Elizabeth the Queen Mother would visit Nova Scotia a number of times, most notably in July 1967 on the occasion of the centenary of the Canadian Confederation.

Queen Elizabeth II has paid several visits to Government House in Nova Scotia, the first as Princess Elizabeth in 1951 during her first Canadian tour with Prince Philip. The Prince of Wales went to Nova Scotia in 1983 with Diana, Princess of Wales, when they stayed on the Royal Yacht *Britannia* in Halifax's harbour, although they were entertained to lunch at Government House by the Lieutenant-Governor of Nova Scotia. In 2014, Prince Charles returned with Camilla, Duchess of Cornwall, when he was sworn in as a Member of the Queen's Privy Council of Canada by the Governor-General of Canada in the drawing room of Government House.

In 2019, the Duke of York visited Government House as Colonel-in-Chief of the Princess Louise Fusiliers, a reserve infantry regiment named after Princess Louise when she lived in Canada as the Vice-Regal Consort, to commemorate the 150th anniversary of the creation of the regiment. Many more members of the Royal Family have attended events at Government House on official visits to Nova Scotia over the years.

Today, Government House stands at 1451 Barrington Street in Halifax, giving it a prominent urban location with small gardens. As one of the oldest official residences in Canada, it was designated as a National Historic Site of Canada in 1982. Government House underwent a three-year C\$6.25 million renovation, which was completed in 2009 in time for Queen Elizabeth II's 2010 visit to Nova Scotia, when she accepted a new royal key to the official residence.

Antiqua Print Gallery/Alamy MHPMXE

Queen's Park, Ontario

The most populous province of Canada, Ontario is the fourth largest of Canada's provinces and territories. Located in east central Canada, the province is bordered by Manitoba to the west, Québec to the east and several states of the United States of America to the south, along many of the Great Lakes. The region was inhabited by numerous indigenous peoples, including the Ojibwa, Cree and Algonquin in the north, and Iroquois and Wyandot people in the south, prior to European settlement. In 1611, the English explorer Henry Hudson sailed into the Hudson Bay to claim the area, but there followed many years of conflict between the French, English and indigenous peoples for the land rights.

The area came to be colonised by the British in the 18th century, although many people displaced from the American Wars of Independence came to settle in the region. The 1791 *Constitutional Act* split the area into Upper Canada to the south-west of the province that is now Ontario, and Lower Canada in what is modern-day Québec.

Colonel John Graves Simcoe was appointed the first Lieutenant-Governor of Upper Canada in 1793. The Lieutenant-Governors of this period lived in houses that were usually part of the military barracks in York, the capital of Upper Canada, named in honour of Prince Frederick, Duke of York, second son of King George III. However, York was renamed and incorporated as the city of Toronto in 1834, becoming the provincial capital of the renamed province of Ontario during the time of the Canadian Confederation in 1867.

Several different properties, including a Regency Italianate villa named Elmsley House, were used as official residences for the Lieutenant-Governors of Ontario during the early part of the 19th century, as the provincial government sought to establish its capital. A new Government House was built in Toronto between 1868 and 1870 in the French Second Empire style, a large residence that became the centre of the social life of the province. Royal visitors during this period included the Marquess of Lorne, Governor-General of Canada, and his wife, Princess Louise, in 1879 and the Duke and Duchess of Cornwall and York (later King George V and Queen Mary) in 1901.

Above right: The former Government House in Toronto played host to many members of the Royal Family between 1870 and 1910.

Canada

The increasing development of the centre of Toronto and the political demands of local Members of Parliament to distance the province of Ontario from its British past led to Government House being sold off to the Canadian Pacific Railway in 1910. The site was later transformed into modern offices and a concert hall that remain today.

However, little more than two years later, construction began on a new Government House at Chorley Park in Toronto, which was to follow the same French-chateau-style typical of the period. Lieutenant-Governor of Ontario, Sir John Hendrie would move into the huge residence at Chorley Park in 1915, which had many official reception rooms, a principal Royal Suite and 22 guest bedrooms. The house welcomed the Prince of Wales (later King Edward VIII) in 1919 and again in 1927 when he visited with his brother, Prince George (later the Duke of Kent), for the Diamond Jubilee anniversary of Canadian Confederation.

The fate of Chorley Park as Government House was to go the same way as its predecessor and the house was closed in 1937 due to the economic climate and the provincial and federal governments' squabbles over official appointments. An auction sale in 1938 sold off over 2,000 furnishings and the building became a military hospital before being demolished in 1961.

With the closing of Chorley Park and the lack of an official residence, the Government of Ontario offered the Lieutenant-Governor of Ontario the use of the Speaker's Apartment and Cabinet Dining Room, which were located at Queen's Park, the Legislative Assembly building of Ontario dating from 1893. Some of the most striking items from Chorley Park were moved to the new Lieutenant-Governor's Suite in the Queen's Park apartment, including six crystal chandeliers, a collection of paintings of Ontario's Lieutenant-Governors and specially commissioned furniture made by the T. Eaton Company.

Left: Government House at Chorley Park in Toronto was the official residence between 1915 and 1937. Sadly it was demolished in 1961.

Historic Collection/Alamy K1DHKR

Above and below right:
The Lieutenant-Governor's
Suite is located at Queen's
Park, the Legislative
Assembly building of
Ontario, and features many
pieces of original furniture
and paintings from the
previous Government
Houses of Ontario.

The Lieutenant-Governor's Suite serves as the setting for formal events and hospitality for the province of Ontario today. The three-storey suite of rooms includes a large drawing room, dining room, music room for larger functions and the Lieutenant-Governor's official office. The suite also has its own entrance.

A small formal rose garden in the grounds of Queen's Park form part of the Legislative Precinct Grounds. The rose garden was originally donated by the Monarchist League of Canada in honour of the Silver Jubilee of Queen Elizabeth II in 1977 and it has subsequently been added to with gardens commemorating the Golden and Diamond Jubilees in 2002 and 2012 respectively.

In 1939, King George VI and Queen Elizabeth visited the suite of the then Lieutenant-Governor of Ontario, Albert Matthews, where he presented the Dionne quintuplets to the royal couple. Born in 1934, the famous Dionne girls from Ontario were the first quintuplets in the world known to have survived their infancy.

Queen Elizabeth II and many other members of the Royal Family have visited the suite at Queen's Park during their official stays in Toronto.

Canada

Government House, Prince Edward Island

Prince Edward Island is the smallest of Canada's Maritime Provinces on the Atlantic Ocean and the province's 2,000 square miles (5,600 square kilometres) and 140,000-strong population is located mainly on the largest island, with over 230 smaller islands surrounding it. The islands were part of the traditional lands of the Mi'kmaq and they became a British colony in the early 1700s. In 1798–99, the islands were named after Prince Edward, Duke of Kent, the fourth son of King George III and the father of Queen Victoria.

In September 1864, Prince Edward Island hosted the Charlottetown Conference, which was seen as the first stage of the creation of Canada in 1867 and is regarded by many to be the 'birthplace of the Confederation', although the province itself didn't join the dominion until 1873, after also considering the idea of either remaining as a British colony or joining the United States of America.

The Canadian monarch is represented by the Lieutenant-Governor of Prince Edward Island whose official residence is Government House, located on an estate often known as Fanningbank, in the province's capital city of Charlottetown. Government House was built between 1832 and 1834 on a piece of land referred to locally as 'Fanning's Bank', which had been set aside in 1789 by then Lieutenant-Governor, Edmund Fanning, for future use as the site of a Vice-Regal residence. Part of the estate later became the city's Victoria Park.

The large, Georgian wood-framed property is widely acknowledged to have been designed by Yorkshire architect, Isaac Smith, who was engaged to build the house along with his brother, Henry Smith, and Nathan Wright. Isaac Smith was later to design Province House, the Legislative Assembly of Prince Edward Island, and both buildings share similar Palladian architectural features, although it is also said that Government House exhibited characteristics of the Greek Revival style that was prevalent in North America at the time.

Above and right: Prince Edward Island's Government House in the province's capital city, Charlottetown, was built between 1832 and 1834.

The cost of building Government House was over £3,100 at the time of construction. Few exterior alterations have been made to the residence since it was built and so it is largely unchanged today.

The sizable entrance hall features a first-floor gallery on four sides supported by eight 15-foot (4.5-metre) high columns and a wide staircase that sweeps up from the back of the hall. The formal dining room contains a mahogany table that seats 24 people for lunches and dinners and was specially made for the residence by Seddon's in London in 1834. Visitors are received in the official reception rooms off the main hall and the first floor has a guest suite and private rooms for the Lieutenant-Governor and their family.

Government House has received many important visitors over the years, beginning with the Prince of Wales (later King Edward VII) in 1860, when a welcome arch was erected opposite the property. This was followed by the 'Fathers of the Confederation', a group of politicians who met at Government House for the Charlottetown Conference in 1864.

Canada

All images: Courtesy of Government House, Prince Edward Island/
Brian L. Simpson, Provincial Photographer, Communications PEI.

Left and below: Government House's formal reception rooms lead from the main entrance hall to the first-floor bedroom suites.

In 1879, the Governor-General of Canada, the Marquess of Lorne, and Princess Louise came to Prince Edward Island, although instead of staying at Government House, they remained on-board their ship in the harbour. During the First World War, Government House became a convalescence home for wounded soldiers and the Lieutenant-Governors of the period moved out to other properties for several years.

In 1939, when King George VI and Queen Elizabeth stayed at Government House in Prince Edward Island during their Canadian royal tour, the planned garden party was called off due to a heavy storm and guests crowded into the residence to take shelter from the torrential downpour. Twenty years later, they were followed by Queen Elizabeth II and Prince Philip, who were welcomed to Government House in 1959 during a royal tour of Canada on the first of several visits – the most notable being in 1964, for the opening of the 'Fathers of the Confederation' Building in Charlottetown.

Government House was designated as a National Historic Site of Canada in 1971 and today it hosts many official functions and ceremonies for the province. The residence is not generally open to the public, except for guided tours in July and August and the traditional New Year's levées, in common with many provinces of Canada, when the Lieutenant-Governor receives local citizens at Government House at the start of the year.

Government House, Saskatchewan

The province of Saskatchewan in central western Canada was originally part of the vast Northwest Territories before it became a separate province in 1905. Settled by Europeans in around 1774, Saskatchewan occupies an area of over 250,000 square miles (650,000 square kilometres) and is surrounded by both Canadian provinces and US states. Today, it has a population of over 1.1 million people and the provincial capital is Regina. The Latin word for 'queen', Regina was said to have been named in honour of Queen Victoria in 1882 by her daughter, Princess Louise, who was in Canada as the Vice-Regal Consort of the Governor-General of Canada, the Marquess of Lorne.

Government House in Regina, Saskatchewan, was the official residence for the Lieutenant-Governor of the Northwest Territories, when the territorial capital was located there before the sub-division of the Territories and Regina became the provincial capital of Saskatchewan. The first brick-built Government House in Regina was erected in 1883 to replace previous wooden houses, although the single-storey house was only used for a few years before a more permanent residence was sought.

A new Government House was constructed between 1889 and 1891 by local contractor

William Henderson to a design by Thomas Fuller, the British-Canadian architect who had been part of the team responsible for the Federal Parliament Buildings in Ottawa in 1866. The new property was built in the Italianate style with a square dome at the centre of the roof and the initials 'VR' above the main entrance for 'Victoria Regina'.

Above and right: Government House in Regina was constructed between 1889 and 1891. The history of the residence is commemorated with a plaque in its grounds.

The extensive interior included a main hall, reception rooms and a dining room, library and guest suites. At the time of completion, Government House was one of the most advanced houses in Regina, with running water drawn from a local well, indoor

Canada

flushing toilets and electrified lighting, as well as being connected to the local telephone exchange over 4-kilometres away. After it was completed at a cost of C$50,000, Joseph Royal, Lieutenant-Governor of the Northwest Territories was the first to live there.

In 1901, the Duke and Duchess of Cornwall and York (later King George V and Queen Mary) stayed at Regina's Government House during their visit to the Northwest Territories. A conservatory was built at Government House in 1901 and a ballroom was later added in 1929.

After Saskatchewan became a separate province in 1905, several royal visitors came to stay. Prince Arthur, Duke of Connaught, visited several times with his wife, the Duchess of Connaught, and their daughter, Princess Patricia, most notably in 1912 when, as Governor-General, he inaugurated the new Saskatchewan Legislative Assembly. The Prince of Wales (later King Edward VIII) went to Saskatchewan in 1919 and 1927. King George VI and Queen Elizabeth travelled there on their royal tour of Canada in 1939, when they visited the University of Saskatchewan. In 1941, the Earl of Athlone, as Governor-General of Canada paid several visits to Regina and the surrounding rural communities of Saskatchewan, accompanied by Princess Alice, Countess of Athlone.

In 1944–45, following the example of Ontario, Government House in Saskatchewan was closed due to the poor economic climate at the end of the Second World War and the effects of drought on agricultural industries in the Canadian Prairie Provinces. The Lieutenant-Governor established a small office at the Hotel Saskatchewan, the grand 1920s hotel opened by the Canadian Pacific Railway, and royal visitors often stayed in one of its guest suites. Many of the furnishings from Government House were sold at auction and the property was leased to the federal government as a home for wartime veterans. The building was also used as an adult education centre under the name of Saskatchewan House and part of the grounds were sold off for development.

Fortunately, in 1968, the former residence was designated a National Historic Site of Canada and local interest groups came together to campaign for its restoration. In 1969, the Society for the Preservation and Restoration of Saskatchewan House (later the Government House Historical Society) was formed. By 1980, Government House had reverted to its original name and many historical contents had been restored to it courtesy of local residents.

In 1984, the offices of the Lieutenant-Governor of Saskatchewan were returned to Government House and many Vice-Regal receptions and events began to be held in the former residence. The role of the restored house was to be a publicly accessible building for the wide use of the province, and so the Lieutenant-Governors have not been provided with accommodation there.

Government House today has developed as a museum and historic centre with guided tours and events. The traditional New Year's Day levée has resumed there with the Lieutenant-Governor of Saskatchewan hosting the annual event. In 2005, a new visitor centre and coach house were added to the building.

Royal visits to Saskatchewan have continued over the decades. Queen Elizabeth II first visited as Princess Elizabeth with Prince Philip in 1951, before returning again in 1959, 1973, 1978 and 1987. In 2005, The Queen went to Government House in Regina to officially open the new wing named in her honour, as well as the Wiebe Interpretive Centre featuring interactive displays and the history of the Crown in Saskatchewan. All four of The Queen's children have also been to Regina at various times as well as many other members of the Royal Family.

Below: Today, Government House in Saskatchewan is a museum and historic centre with guided tours and regular events.

Jimmy S. Emerson

Northwest Territories

The Northwest Territories is a federal territory of Canada and the second-largest of the three most sparsely populated territories of Canada, with a population of just under 45,000 people.

The history of the vast Northwest Territories began with the First Nations peoples, who lived in the area before the European settlers arrived in the 16th and 17th centuries. The region went through many different administrative stages and was divided into the provinces of Alberta, Saskatchewan and Manitoba, the territories of Yukon and Nunavut, and finally the remaining area of the Northwest Territories.

The Canadian monarch is not directly represented in the region and the Commissioner of the Northwest Territories is the Federal Government of Canada's representative. The Commissioner undertakes similar ceremonial functions to the Lieutenant-Governors in other Canadian provinces and territories, but there is no historic Vice-Regal official residence in the Northwest Territories' capital of Yellowknife.

Queen Elizabeth II has visited the Northwest Territories three times, although it would have been four had she not been suffering from suspected morning sickness while pregnant with Prince Andrew, during her 1959 Canadian tour. Prince Philip deputised for The Queen on that trip to Yellowknife.

However, The Queen did eventually visit Northwest Territories in 1970, along with Prince Philip and two of her children, Prince Charles and Princess Anne, and she came again in 1994 and 2002, by which time Nunavut had separated from the Northwest Territories.

Nunavut

Nunavut is the newest, largest and northernmost territory of Canada, which separated officially from the Northwest Territories in 1999. It is one of the world's most remote and sparsely populated areas, with a population of just over 35,000 people inhabiting a region of over 680,000 square miles (1.9 million square kilometres).

The Commissioner of Nunavut is the Federal Government of Canada's representative in the territory and undertakes similar ceremonial functions to the Lieutenant-Governors in Canadian provinces. Like the Northwest Territories, the Canadian monarch is not represented directly in Nunavut and there is no historic Vice-Regal official residence in the capital, Iqaluit.

Queen Elizabeth II and Prince Philip visited Nunavut in 2002 as part of the Canadian leg of their Golden Jubilee tour of the Commonwealth, when they went to the Legislative buildings in Iqaluit. The Queen had been there before during her 1970 Canadian tour when the territory was previously part of the Northwest Territories.

Canada

Images: Courtesy of the Office of the Commissioner of Yukon

Commissioner's Residence, Yukon

Yukon is the most westerly of Canada's three federal territories and it has the smallest population with under 36,000 people. The territory was divided from the Northwest Territories in 1898 and became part of the Confederation of Canada.

The Commissioner of Yukon is the Federal Government of Canada's representative and today undertakes similar ceremonial functions to the Lieutenant-Governors in Canadian provinces, though earlier Commissioners had a more involved role in the administration of the territory.

Built in 1901 in Dawson City by architect Thomas Fuller, the original Commissioner's residence was a three-storey timber house with covered verandahs inspired by Arts and Crafts design. As the official home of the Commissioner of Yukon, it was sometimes known as Government House.

Above left and left: The original Commissioner's residence was built in 1901 in Dawson City. The interior of the former official residence is largely intact from the period and today it is used for formal and informal functions.

The house was in use until 1916, when it ceased to be the formal residence. Since then it has been utilised in various different ways, including as an old people's home. The property was acquired by Parks Canada in 1973 and was added to the Classified Federal Heritage list as a historical building.

The interior is largely intact from the period and the building is now a National Historic Site, open seasonally to the public. The former Commissioner's Residence is used regularly for official functions, receptions and presentations, giving local people the opportunity to enjoy this historic house.

Taylor House

Since 2015, the Commissioner of Yukon has used Taylor House as an official office in Whitehorse, Yukon's capital city since 1953 when it moved from Dawson City. The log-built property was constructed in 1937 as a residence for Bill and Aline Taylor, who were local citizens and business people. Their home was designed by Aline Taylor and it features many architectural influences, including American Arts and Crafts, and Colonial Revival styles. Taylor House is a local landmark in the historic downtown area of Whitehorse.

Above right and right: Taylor House was inaugurated in 2015 as the official office for the Commissioner of Yukon in Whitehorse, Yukon's capital city.

Canada

Images: Courtesy of the Office of the Commissioner of Yukon

Government House, Grenada

The island of Grenada is a Commonwealth realm in the south-east Caribbean Sea, often known as the 'Spice Island' due to its exports of locally-grown nutmeg and mace. The main island covers an area of 134 square miles (349 square kilometres) and, together with six smaller islands, Grenada has a population of around 110,000 people.

Before the arrival of European settlers in the Caribbean, the indigenous Arawaks and Caribs lived in Grenada. It is said that explorer Christopher Columbus sighted the island in 1498 on his voyages to the Americas. The French settled in Grenada around 1650 until the islands were ceded to the British as part of the settlement of the Treaty of Paris in 1763. Grenada became independent in 1974.

Above left: A photograph of Government House in Grenada from around c1963 shows the fine residence as it originally looked with its verandahs that had views over the harbour of St George's.

Left: The island of Grenada was hit by the powerful Hurricane Ivan in September 2004, which left Government House seriously damaged and an uninhabitable shell. However, many original features of the former official residence are still visible today.

Between 1763 and 1974, the Crown was represented in Grenada by a succession of Governors and Administrators. When Grenada became independent and a Commonwealth realm in 1974, the sovereign's representative was given the title of Governor-General.

The official residence of Grenada was Government House for many generations, though little is known about its origins. Initially a wooden house near the main harbour and capital of St George's, when the British Governor of Grenada arrived in 1784, Government House was established at the Mount St George estate overlooking the harbour. The estate was purchased from William Lucas for £20,000, and in the early 1800s, the house was enlarged and extended into a two-storey Georgian villa. Between 1887 and 1888, Government House was remodelled, with the addition of an elaborate two-storey verandah. In the 1920s, a further gallery was constructed above the verandah.

Several members of the Royal Family visited Government House in Grenada, including Princess Margaret on her Caribbean tour in 1955, and Queen Elizabeth II and Prince Philip in 1985, when they were also invited to the Parliament of Grenada, which at that time was located at York House in St George's.

Government House was the setting for one of Grenada's most dangerous moments in recent history, when US Navy SEALs parachuted into the gardens of the residence to rescue Governor-General, Sir Paul Scoon and his wife Esmai, in October 1983. This followed a period of political unrest in the country lasting several years, after a coup d'état and revolution in 1979. American troops helped to restore calm on the island, though many other nations criticised the intervention of the United States in an independent Commonwealth country.

After nearly 50 years being largely spared from the destructive impact of the many hurricanes from the Atlantic Ocean that affect the Caribbean region, the island of Grenada was hit by the powerful Hurricane Ivan in September 2004. Government House was seriously damaged, leaving an uninhabitable shell of a former residence that had to be abandoned. Today, the Governor-General of Grenada conducts official engagements from a small office in St George's and lives in a property elsewhere on the island.

The historic Parliament of Grenada at York House in St George's was also amongst the many buildings destroyed in the 2004 hurricane. After a long period of reinvestment and redevelopment of the island, a new modern US$15 million Grenada Parliament building was opened in 2018, at a site near to the former Government House overlooking St George's.

The new Parliament building was officially opened with the unveiling of plaques by the Governor-General of Grenada, Dame Cécile La Grenade, and the Prime Minister of Grenada, Dr Keith Mitchell. The parliamentary chamber has a large, wooden ceiling design in the

Grenada

shape of a nutmeg pod, reflecting the island's spice trade history. The project was financially supported by the governments of Mexico, the United Arab Emirates and Australia.

The Parliament building is the most recent and modern public structure in Grenada, and has been admired by many locals and visitors alike. The development is part of a regeneration project for an area of the island that will include tourist attractions.

In 2019, the Prince of Wales and the Duchess of Cornwall visited the new Parliament buildings in St George's and the Prince also went to the nearby ruins of Government House, where he viewed the former residence and planted a tree in the grounds.

It is hoped that the former Government House will one day receive the investment required to restore this historic residence to its former glory.

Below: The historic, former Parliament of Grenada at York House in St George's (left) was amongst many buildings destroyed in the 2004 hurricane. The new, modern Grenada Parliament building (right) was opened in 2018 at a site near to the former Government House on a hill overlooking St George's.

Grenada

King's House, Jamaica

One of the largest island realms of the Commonwealth, Jamaica lies at the heart of the Caribbean Sea and has a population of nearly 3 million people. The island covers over 4,000 square miles (10,000 square kilometres).

Following the arrival of early settlers including Christopher Columbus in 1494, the region was ruled by the Spanish and was known as the Colony of Santiago. Tragically, many of the indigenous Arawak and Taino peoples of the islands were killed or died of diseases to which they had no immunity during this period. In 1655, the English settled on the island and renamed it Jamaica. The plantation economy grew rapidly at this time, with many people from West Africa transported as slaves to the island, while the sugar and rum from the plantations was traded across the globe. This trade continued until the abolition of slavery in Jamaica in 1834 with emancipation four years later. During the 19th and 20th centuries, Jamaica was a Crown Colony before it became independent from the United Kingdom on 6 August 1962 as an independent Commonwealth realm. The British monarch was represented over the years by a succession of Commanders, Governors and Lieutenant-Governors, until Jamaica became a constitutional monarchy in 1962 and the Jamaican head of state was represented by the Governor-General.

One of the earliest Governor's houses was located in Port Royal, a large settlement port on the island, and was used by the Governors of Jamaica in the late 17th century. However, the first official residence was constructed in 1762 in Spanish Town, the designated capital of Jamaica. Plans for the property in Spanish Town were drawn up by Thomas Craskell, the Chief Engineer at the time. The formal homes of the Governors of Jamaica have always been called King's House, with the name not changing to Queen's House even during the reign of Queens. The large Palladian mansion in Spanish Town was the centre of national life for nearly a hundred years before the capital of Jamaica moved to Kingston in 1872. The 'Old King's House' in Spanish Town, as it later came to be known, was for a time used as The Queen's College after the Governor moved out, but sadly it fell victim to a large fire in 1925 which destroyed many original features. Today, the building is a historic ruin and museum.

The Governors of Jamaica required a residence in the new capital of Kingston and so it was decided to build a new King's House at the site of Bishop's Lodge, the traditional home of the Anglican Lord Bishop of the Diocese of Jamaica, also known as Somerset Pen. The property and estate were purchased for the Crown in 1871, but the final amount paid

Above: 'Old King's House' in Spanish Town was the official residence of the Governor in Jamaica for nearly a hundred years before the capital moved to Kingston in 1872. Today the building is a historic ruin and museum.

Jamaica

was ultimately disputed and it is thought to have been between £3,000 and £5,000. King's House was built around the former Bishop's Lodge at a cost of £8,000, but unfortunately the new building was partially destroyed by an earthquake in 1907. Although the house and outbuildings suffered from a further fire in 1908, the present King's House has retained many of the architectural features of the original property when it was remodelled by the British architect, Sir Charles Nicholson in the same year.

Today, King's House is the main residence and office for the Governor-General of Jamaica and it hosts many state and official ceremonies. It is a large three-storey property, with a unique style and is usually painted white. The ground floor is arranged around a large open patio with reception rooms for official entertaining. The foyer has three silver lamps on display presented by the British Government to mark Jamaica's independence in 1962. The ballroom features portraits of successive monarchs and past Governors of Jamaica. The dining room, one of the only original rooms to survive the 1907 earthquake along with a side annex, served as the chapel when the house was the Bishop's Lodge and there is evidence of its religious architectural features from its time as a place of worship.

The office of the Governor-General is located on the first floor of King's House and includes a drawing room and morning room, each with a mixture of antique and modern furniture. The drawing room contains hurricane globe chandeliers adorned with golden leaves, which were original items brought from 'Old King's House' in Spanish Town. The morning room has a collection of antique 19th-century ceremonial silverware and military memorabilia belonging to the West India Regiment. The top floor of the house has the master bedroom suite and residential space for the Governor-General and official guests.

King's House has beautiful gardens that were originally laid out in 1907–08 under then Governor, Sir John Peter Grant, as well as over 150-acres (60-hectares) of lush sub-tropical estate. The grounds have a mile-long driveway flanked by palms, named somewhat obviously Palm Tree Avenue, and they also feature many outstanding flora and fauna, including huge cotton trees imported from South Africa, said to have been planted in 1779, and several trees planted by various royal visitors over the years. In 1973, another property called Jamaica House was built on 30-acres (12-hectares) of land divided from the King's House estate, for use as the official residence of the Prime Minister of Jamaica, although it has also served as an official Office of the Prime Minister when the prime ministerial home has been elsewhere.

Many members of the Royal Family have visited Jamaica and King's House over the years. One of the earliest occasions was in 1861 when Prince Alfred, Duke of Edinburgh, came to Jamaica and stayed at the residence in Spanish Town. Sadly, his time there was cut short when the news arrived that Queen Victoria's mother and the Prince's grandmother, the Duchess of Kent, had died and he had to return home.

In 1891, Prince George of Wales (later King George V) visited Kingston to open the Jamaica International Exhibition, which was modelled on the 1851 Great Exhibition in London and designed to boost Jamaican trade. The Duke and Duchess of York (later King George VI

Below: Today, King's House is the main residence and office for the Governor-General of Jamaica, and it hosts many state functions and official ceremonies.

and Queen Elizabeth) came to Jamaica during overseas tours in 1927 and again in 1931. Prince George, Duke of Kent and his wife, Princess Marina, Duchess of Kent, visited King's House on their honeymoon in 1935 and the occasion is commemorated by a tree they planted in the gardens.

One of the more regular royal visitors to King's House was Princess Alice, Countess of Athlone, the last surviving grandchild of Queen Victoria. In 1950, the Princess was elected, on the recommendation of King George VI, to become Chancellor of the University College of the West Indies in Kingston, Jamaica, shortly after its foundation. The Princess would combine her annual duties at the university's graduation ceremonies with a winter holiday in the Caribbean each year, staying at King's House.

Above: King's House has beautiful gardens covering over 150-acres and featuring many outstanding flora and fauna.

The first visit by a reigning monarch to Jamaica was made during the 1953–54 Coronation tour of the Commonwealth by Queen Elizabeth II and the Duke of Edinburgh. The Queen has returned to Jamaica several times, notably in 1994 and 2002, and stayed at King's House. During the 2002 visit, King's House unfortunately suffered a power cut just as the state banquet was about to begin and The Queen and Prince Philip were led into the dining room to greet over 100 guests by lantern and candlelight.

The Queen was represented by her sister, Princess Margaret, in Jamaica in 1962 when the Princess attended the country's independence celebrations and the opening of the Jamaican Parliament with her husband, the Earl of Snowdon. Both Princess Margaret and Princess Anne also spent part of their honeymoons in Jamaica, in 1960 and 1973 respectively. Prince Harry represented The Queen during the Diamond Jubilee tour of Jamaica when he stayed at King's House in 2012.

The official residence of the Governor-General of Jamaica, King's House is today managed by the Governor-General of Jamaica Trust and the house has been designated as a Historic House and National Monument by the Jamaica Heritage Trust. It hosts hundreds of people for formal functions and ceremonies each year.

Jamaica

Government House, Wellington

The Commonwealth realm of New Zealand is a sovereign nation in the south-west Pacific Ocean and is made up of two main islands, the North Island and the South Island, as well as over 600 smaller islands. Due to its remoteness in the world, New Zealand has developed a unique biodiversity of animals and plant life. The indigenous peoples of New Zealand were Polynesian people who developed a distinctive Maori culture. In the Maori language, New Zealand is known as *Aotearoa*, translated as the 'land of the long white cloud'.

In 1642, the Dutch explorer, Abel Tasman became the first European to sight New Zealand. It was initially named 'Staten Land' but Dutch cartographers later renamed it *Nova Zeelandia*, after the Dutch province of Zeeland. It was said that British explorer James Cook later anglicised the name to New Zealand in the late 18th century, when European settlement in New Zealand was established. New Zealand was initially part of the British colony of New South Wales in Australia.

With growing unrest amongst the different groups in New Zealand, a British naval officer, Captain William Hobson, was sent to negotiate a settlement with local people and in 1840, representatives of the British Crown and the Maori chiefs signed the Treaty of Waitangi, which declared British sovereignty over the islands. The first capital of New Zealand was Okiato (also known as Old Russell) in the northern Bay of Islands, but in 1841, the new city of Auckland was declared as the capital. New Zealand grew rapidly with immigration from the United Kingdom, in particular, in the 19th century and today, the diverse population is around 4.9 million people, mainly of European, Maori, Asian and Pacific ancestry.

In 1865, Wellington, on the southernmost point of the North Island, became New Zealand's capital city and the seat of government. In 1907, New Zealand became a British Dominion before it gained full independence as a nation and as a constitutional monarchy with the passing of the Statute of Westminster in 1947. Since 1840, the Crown in New Zealand has been represented by a series of Governors and later, following independence, by Governors-General of New Zealand, which continues today.

Hidden away in the quiet suburb of Newtown in New Zealand's capital city, Government House, Wellington is the official residence of the Governor-General, the personal representative of the New Zealand sovereign. It is also the formal home of the monarch and the Royal Family when they are in New Zealand. The quiet and unassuming entrance sets

Above: Built in the Edwardian period, this Arts and Crafts-style Government House occupies a beautiful location in the city of Wellington and has been at the heart of New Zealand's official life since 1910.

the tone of this Vice-Regal residence. Wellington is a city that doesn't stand on too much formality and Government House is no exception. A long driveway leads up to the main residence, with the 30-acres (12-hectares) of beautiful gardens shared with the nearby Wellington College.

This was not the first Government House in Wellington. The original official residence was a plain single-storey villa built for

Colonel William Wakefield, the British Agent for the New Zealand Company, in 1840. Although the house was used as a hospital for a time after a major earthquake in 1848, there is a record of the first Government House Ball being held there on 10 February 1849. The property was sometimes referred to as Government House or Wakefield House, although the capital city at the time was still Auckland and the Wellington abode played a lesser role in the official life of the nation.

The second Government House in Wellington was built in 1868 on land adjacent to the new Parliament Buildings, shortly after the capital city was moved to Wellington. A large timber-built mansion was constructed in the Italianate style, similar to Queen Victoria's Osborne House. This property was designed by William Henry Clayton, and when it was completed in 1871, it had fine views across the harbour. The house was the official residence of ten successive Governors of New Zealand until 1907, when a fire in the main Parliament Buildings resulted in Government House being used as a parliamentary debating chamber. This led to a new third Government House being commissioned in its own private grounds. The second residence later became a parliamentary restaurant, before being demolished in 1969 when it was replaced by the distinctive 'Beehive' modern building of the New Zealand Parliament.

Right: The formal lawn at the rear of the house has been the setting for receiving many Heads of State and official visitors with both a New Zealand Armed Forces military band and a traditional Maori welcoming ceremony.

New Zealand

The third and current Government House was built in Wellington between 1908 and 1910 and was designed in the office of the main government architect of the time, John Campbell (who was also responsible for New Zealand's Parliament Buildings), although his assistant, Claude Paton, is largely credited with designing Government House. It is a large, handsome Edwardian residence with eight guest suites, 27 bedrooms and 19 bathrooms, including staff quarters, covering over 45,000 square feet (4,100 square metres). The official residence was designed in an Arts and Crafts style with a half-timbered Tudor frontage. The mix of styles was intended to evoke the look of an English country residence with a flag tower rising from the roof.

One of the only major additions to the property's exterior over the years is the garden terrace leading down to the formal lawn at the rear of the house, which is used for receiving Heads of State and official visitors with the attendance of a military band and a traditional Maori welcoming ceremony on the lawn.

The main entrance, known as the 'Taupaepae', is where guests arrive and it features the stained-glass insignia of King George V (the King-Emperor at the time the house was completed in 1910) and the wood-carved coats of arms of former Governors-General who have lived at Government House. The main hall also contains two traditional wood-carved 'pou', or pillar facings, in the Taranaki style, reflecting the Maori heritage of New Zealand.

Unfortunately, neither King George V nor his son, King George VI, were able to visit Government House in Wellington (King George VI and Queen Elizabeth's planned tour in 1949 was cancelled due to ill health) and so the first reigning monarch to stay in the residence as New Zealand monarch was Queen Elizabeth II, accompanied by the Duke of Edinburgh during their Coronation tour of 1953–54. It is fitting, therefore, that the largest room in the house, the Ballroom, is dominated by the 1960 portrait of Queen Elizabeth II by Denis Fildes, which hangs above two royal thrones and is lit by two bright Czech-made crystal chandeliers. There is also a large portrait of Queen Victoria on permanent loan from the Royal Collection at Windsor Castle on display in the Ballroom. This is the main formal room in the house and as such it is used for investitures, concerts and ceremonial occasions.

Above and opposite page: The largest room at Government House is the Ballroom, dominated by its portraits of Queen Victoria and Queen Elizabeth II.

All images Courtesy of the Office of the Governor-General of New Zealand

Next door is the L-shaped, interconnecting drawing room used by the Governor-General to receive visiting Heads of State and also for the visits of foreign ambassadors who come to Government House to present their credentials. The two rooms, today known as the Blundell Drawing Room and the Porritt Room, are light and elegant with formal but comfortable furniture. On her 2002 visit to New Zealand, The Queen held a small reception for the media in the formal drawing room and it was said that the Governor-General's amused staff watched as the 'cynical and often republican' journalists and newspaper editors were charmed by the sovereign.

The grand piano in one corner of the drawing room is covered in official signed photographs of the various royal visitors to the house – including The Queen and Prince Philip, the Princess Royal and Prince Edward, the Earl of Wessex. There is also a photograph of the Emperor and Empress of Japan, who stayed at Government House when they were Crown Prince Naruhito and Crown Princess Masako on one of the latter's rare overseas visits. The room also contains one of the most historic paintings in the residence, the only known portrait of Captain James Cook's close friend, Captain Charles Clerke, painted by Sir Nathaniel Dance in 1776.

Informal lunch parties or small receptions are often held in the beautiful, light Bledisloe Conservatory, which is entered via the drawing room, and commands fine views of the gardens and the city of Wellington in the distance.

The main corridor runs almost the whole length of the house and is covered with a bright red carpet that was only recently replaced after

Right: The Blundell Drawing Room is used to receive guests and for small meetings or receptions.

New Zealand

Left: The Norrie State Dining Room at Government House in Wellington features an extending, mahogany table dating from 1880 and 22 tapestry chairs around the table, part of a set of 38 chairs, each representing the principal towns and cities of New Zealand.

50 years of service. The original carpet had been commissioned in preparation for King George VI's planned royal visit that was later cancelled due to ill health. The corridor is hung with portraits and caricatures of all of the former Governors-General of New Zealand, along with their coats of arms, and there is also a selection of fine gifts on display from the many visitors to the house. These include a diamond-encrusted cigar box from the Sultan of Brunei, a gold apple covered in precious stones from the Crown Prince of Brunei and a beautiful porcelain tea set from Prince Edward.

There are a number of official rooms leading from the main corridor, including the Governor-General's study and a small private dining room known as the Fitzroy Room. The Liverpool Room, named after the Earl of Liverpool (who was Governor-General between 1912 and 1920), is a smaller, somewhat less formal room often used for bilateral meetings with visiting dignitaries or for serving afternoon tea to modest-sized groups.

Until the early 1970s, the Executive Council of New Zealand, headed by the Governor-General, met in the Council Room at Government House, although today it convenes at the Parliament Buildings. The Council Room is now used for business and charity meetings.

Further along the main corridor is the Norrie State Dining Room, used by the Governor-General for entertaining on a grand scale. This formal room has the feeling of a large English country house and the extending, mahogany table dates from 1880. There are 22 tapestry chairs around the table, part of a set of 38 chairs at Government House, each representing the principal towns and cities of New Zealand. They were embroidered in the 1950s by the Country Women's Institute of New Zealand when it was discovered that the dining room was in need of chairs. The four carver chairs (with arms) are embroidered with the coats of arms of the four major cities of New Zealand: Auckland, Wellington, Christchurch and Dunedin. Each successive Governor-General had previously brought their own furniture to the house, which was removed when they departed, so there were very few original pieces of furniture in the house.

The State Dining Room is hung with portraits from the Norrie Collection of artworks. These remarkable portraits were given to the people of New Zealand by the Governor-General, Lord Norrie, and his wife in 1957. The collection contains many paintings of royalty from the Houses of Tudor and Stuart, as well as a portrait of Oliver Cromwell. The

State Dining Room also features a beautiful model of a 16ᵗʰ-century galleon from King Juan Carlos of Spain and two silver pheasants from Queen Beatrix of the Netherlands, who both stayed at Government House during official visits to New Zealand.

In 2008, after almost a century of use, Government House closed for major strengthening and renovation work, costing more than NZ$40 million, to ensure the residence's future survival. The three-year project saw extensive work on the structure and interior of the house, including using the latest technology to make the house 'earthquake proof'. One of the major elements of the refurbishment was the replacement of the flooring in the official rooms with newly designed carpets being created by New Zealand artists that incorporated symbols like the traditional silver fern. During the renovation work between 2008 and 2011, the Governor-General's formal home was moved to Vogel House, renamed Government House Vogel for the period, in the suburb of Lower Hutt, north of the capital. The timber house was built in 1932 as a wedding gift for Jocelyn Riddiford from her parents when she married James Vogel and, in 1966, the property was gifted to the government for use as an official residence.

The grounds of Government House in Wellington extend to 30-acres (12-hectares) and feature a range of different garden landscapes and mature trees, as well as tennis courts, a Second World War bomb shelter and a new visitor centre opened by the Prince of Wales, which was New Zealand's Diamond Jubilee gift to The Queen in 2012.

Recent royal visitors to Government House during several tours of New Zealand have been the Prince of Wales and the Duchess of Cornwall, the Duke and Duchess of Cambridge, and the Duke and Duchess of Sussex, who all planted trees in the grounds to mark their visits. In 2014, the Duke and Duchess of Cambridge unveiled a new portrait of The Queen by New Zealand artist, Nick Cuthell. Almost all members of the present Royal Family have visited Government House over the years, as well as many overseas monarchs. In 2016, King Willem-Alexander and Queen Maxima of the Netherlands stayed at Government House during their visit to New Zealand and attended a state dinner given in their honour.

Although it is the official residence of the Governor-General of New Zealand, Government House in Wellington is today seen by over 20,000 public visitors a year, who come to attend open days, investitures, receptions and garden parties, as well as annual open days. The house has occupied a unique position for more than a century and continues to be at the heart of ceremonial life in New Zealand.

Right: Portraits of previous monarchs feature prominently at Government House. Along the main staircase hang portraits of King Edward VII and Queen Alexandra, and King George V and Queen Mary.

New Zealand

Phil Braithwaite

Government House, Auckland

The largest city of New Zealand, Auckland, on the North Island, was the capital city between 1841 and 1865 before the seat of government moved to Wellington. However, the city has retained its importance in New Zealand's public and cultural life.

There have been four Vice-Regal residences in Auckland. The first Government House in Auckland was a prefabricated wooden house used by the first Governor of New Zealand, Captain William Hobson, in 1841, but it was later destroyed by fire in 1848. A second Government House was sought and, although it was a rented property, the property was designated as the official residence at the time. This second house was variously known as St Keven's, St Kevin's or Moleskin Hall, although some historians argue that as it was rented then it should not be counted as an official residence. Unfortunately, the house also burnt down in 1857.

The third Government House, today known as Old Government House, was built in 1856 by William Mason. A large, imposing, Italianate residence, it served as the main Vice-Regal home for several years in the late 19th and early 20th centuries, until the capital moved to Wellington, when it became the second residence of the Governor and later, the Governor-General of New Zealand.

Phil Braithwaite

During Queen Elizabeth II's visit to New Zealand as the first reigning monarch to go to the country, she stayed at Old Government House in Auckland with the Duke of Edinburgh in December 1953, as part of the 1953–54 Coronation tour. It was during this stay that The Queen broadcast her Christmas radio message to the Commonwealth from Old Government House, as well as hosting a garden party and children's party in the grounds.

Above left and left: Old Government House was built in 1856 and is today part of the University of Auckland.

Right: Government House in Auckland, New Zealand, was built around 1920 and is surrounded by beautiful landscaped gardens dating from the late 19th century.

Old Government House was eventually taken over by the University of Auckland in 1969 as part of the Auckland City Campus. Initially, it proved difficult to maintain and there were many challenges in maintaining it, however today, the building has been restored and is used as a heritage venue for university events and meetings.

The replacement fourth and current Government House in Auckland was presented to the New Zealand Crown in 1962 by Sir Frank and Lady Ruby Mappin. The large suburban residence is in the district of Mount Eden and it was built around 1920, although the landscaped gardens date from the late 19th century. The property was bought in 1921 by horticulturist and philanthropist, Sir Frank Mappin and his wife, Lady Ruby Mappin, who developed the landscaped gardens and the charming Art Deco house. They named it 'Birchlands' after a previous home they had owned in England. In 1962, the Mappins presented the house to the New Zealand Crown as a future Government House in Auckland to replace the decaying Victorian, Old Government House, although the Mappins continued to live at the house until 1969.

This residence, with its outstanding gardens, is Auckland's present-day Government House. It has the feel of a large suburban property rather than an official residence. It is unique in that there are very few, long-established gardens of its kind that have survived in New Zealand. The grounds have been endorsed as a 'Garden of National Significance' by the New Zealand Gardens Trust. The grounds feature many of the oldest trees in the country, as well as unique flora and fauna. A tall, modern, bronze sculpture titled the 'Splint', designed by Christopher Braddock, stands in front of the house, a gift from former Governor-General of New Zealand, Dame Silvia Cartwright (2001–06), and her husband, Peter Cartwright.

In 2005, a new Government House Pavilion was added to the residence in Auckland by leading heritage architects, Salmond Reed. The pavilion was designed to add a new space to meet the demand for increased official usage, such as welcome ceremonies for overseas visitors as well as state dinners and receptions. The pavilion faces onto the large lawn area for outdoor ceremonies and it is also linked to the main 1920s residence.

Many members of the Royal Family have stayed at Government House in Auckland during their official visits to the city. The one-year-old Prince William was famously photographed by the media during a photocall in the gardens with his parents, the Prince and Princess of Wales, on their New Zealand tour in 1983. At the time, Prince William was the first royal baby to go on an official overseas tour.

New Zealand

Chameleons Eye/Shutterstock 1048187401

Government House, Cook Islands

The Commonwealth realm of New Zealand includes the New Zealand mainland and its Overseas Territories. The Ross Dependency is the area of the Antarctic continent that is part of New Zealand and has no permanent inhabitants; Tokelau is a small island and non-self-governing dependent territory in the southern Pacific Ocean; and Niue is a small, self-governing territory north-east of New Zealand; in all three areas, the New Zealand monarch is represented by the Governor-General of New Zealand.

However, the Cook Islands, also in the southern Pacific Ocean and with a population of over 20,000 people, is a self-governing territory in 'free association' with New Zealand since 1965, meaning that the islands have their own government and parliament but work with the New Zealand government on foreign affairs and defence.

The Queen's Representative in the Cook Islands is the formal title given to the representative of the New Zealand monarch and is a separate office holder to that of the Governor-General of New Zealand. By convention, the appointment of the monarch's representative is made by the New Zealand Crown upon the recommendation of the Prime Minister of the Cook Islands.

There has been an official Vice-Regal residence in the Cook Islands, known as Government House, in the capital of Rarotonga since the early 20th century. Today, the property is a two-storey colonial-style house with covered verandahs and a formal lawn in front of the house. The residence is found in an area known as Titikaveka.

Due to its remoteness, royal visits to the Cook Islands have been rare. Queen Elizabeth II and Prince Philip visited the Cook Islands in 1974, accompanied by Princess Anne and her first husband, Captain Mark Phillips. The main purpose of the trip was for The Queen to open Rarotonga International Airport, en route to New Zealand for the 1974 Commonwealth Games in Christchurch.

Cook Islands

Image courtesy of Government House Papua New Guinea

Government House, Papua New Guinea

The Commonwealth realm of Papua New Guinea occupies the eastern half of the island of New Guinea and its offshore islands in the Pacific Ocean, north of Australia. The western half of New Guinea forms the Indonesian provinces of Papua and West Papua. Papua New Guinea has a largely rural population of 8.6 million people spread across the remote island. The capital of Papua New Guinea is Port Moresby on the south eastern coast.

The islands were settled by Europeans in the late 19th century, although the indigenous population has a history stretching back thousands of years. Germany, Britain and Australia governed the islands in succession until Papua New Guinea established its sovereignty in 1975. Papua New Guinea retained the British and Australian monarch as its head of state. The Governor-General of Papua New Guinea is the Vice-Regal representative of Queen Elizabeth II, who herself is known in 'Tok Pisin', the local pidgin language, as 'Missis Kwin'. Unlike many other Commonwealth realms, the Governor-General is nominated by the national Parliament of Papua New Guinea, rather than being proposed by the Prime Minister.

A Government House has existed in Papua New Guinea since the late 1800s but the present property was built in 1913 and today is the home and office of the Governor-General of Papua New Guinea. The grounds of Government House are unique in the Commonwealth in that they contain two official buildings – Government House, the official residence of the Governor-General and State House, which is used for formal receptions and ceremonies.

Above: The grounds of Government House are unique in the Commonwealth in that they contain two official buildings – Government House, the official residence of the Governor-General (on the left) and State House (on the right), used for official receptions and formal ceremonies.

Government House is located on a hill in a suburb of the capital of Papua New Guinea called Konedobu, which overlooks the local village and former Fairfax Harbour in downtown Port Moresby. When Papua New Guinea attained independence in 1975, Port Moresby was confirmed as its capital. The site of Government House was chosen by Sir Peter Scratchley, the Special Commissioner for the Protectorate of British New Guinea, who arrived in Port Moresby on 28 August 1885. The formal home of the Vice-Regal representative has remained there ever since and the property enjoys beautiful views of the harbour.

Papua New Guinea

Images courtesy of Government House Papua New Guinea

Left: State House is today the location for many of the ceremonial events that take place in Papua New Guinea.

In 1913, Australian born, Sir Hubert Murray, who was the Acting Administrator of the then Territory of Papua, and also Lieutenant-Governor from 1909 to 1940, was responsible for the construction of Government House as an official residence. The design was that of a typical north Queensland station homestead, with a central living room, bedrooms with French-style doors opening into them and a wide verandah completely encircling the house. The building of Government House was a result of typical construction methods adopted in tropical Australia at the time.

It was at Government House that many important decisions were made regarding the future of the British and Australian colony, both administratively and politically. Though not yet unified as a country, both Papua and New Guinea referred to Government House as their Government headquarters.

Many dramatic and historical events would also take place there. In 1904, in front of the old Government House building was a flagpole where then Acting Lieutenant-Governor, Christopher Robinson, had sadly committed suicide after he was criticized for his handling of the investigation into the massacres of two British missionaries, James Chalmers and

Left: The grounds of Government House with the Governor-General of Papua New Guinea's personal standard flying from the flagpole and the views of the harbour beyond.

Above left: The Governor-General of Papua New Guinea and Grand Chief, Sir Bob Dadae conducting an investiture ceremony and conferring a knighthood on recipient, Sir Christopher Charles Abel, at State House.

Above right: The Governor-General receives the new Ambassador of the United States of America to Papua New Guinea, Erin McKee at Government House in November 2019.

Oliver Tomkins. The two Christian missionaries had been imprisoned, cooked and eaten by local tribes at Goaribari Island in the Gulf province in 1901. The subsequent botched investigation and arrest of suspects by the Acting Lieutenant-Governor Robinson resulted in local dissent and criticism from the colonial government which later led to his suicide.

In the valley below Government House, the original barracks of the Royal Papuan Constabulary had once stood, and this was also the location where the US Army had built offices when Government House had been taken over as the military headquarters for General Douglas MacArthur. General MacArthur was known for pacing the corridors of the Vice-Regal residence while giving out orders to his troops fighting the Japanese in the Pacific during the Second World War.

In 1952, Brigadier-General Sir Donald Cleland became the Administrator of the Territory of Papua and New Guinea. Sir Donald and his wife, Lady Rachel, set about redesigning and extending the gardens in and around both Government House and State House, bringing in plants and flowers from all over the country to create the beautiful grounds that flourish today.

Queen Elizabeth II and Prince Philip, Duke of Edinburgh, visited Papua New Guinea for the first time in 1974, accompanied by Princess Anne and her husband, Captain Mark Phillips. The Queen and Prince Philip returned in 1977, as part of their Silver Jubilee tour of the Commonwealth on the Royal Yacht *Britannia*, and again in 1982.

Prince Charles first travelled to Papua New Guinea as a student in Australia in the 1960s and became fascinated by its unique culture. He has visited several times, notably in 1975 when the country celebrated its independence, in 1984 when he opened the new Parliament House, and again with his wife, Camilla, Duchess of Cornwall, during their Diamond Jubilee tour of the region on behalf of The Queen in 2012.

Since 1975, when Papua New Guinea gained independence and chose to retain The Queen as the head of state, Government House has retained its place as the official residence of the Governor-General and at the heart of the ceremonial life of the nation. During the past 45 years, successive government officials, including Prime Ministers, State Ministers and statutory organisations, have come to Government House to be sworn into office by the Governor-General.

The Governor-General also receives overseas heads of missions, High Commissioners and Ambassadors before they take up their positions in the country. The Vice-Regal representative also conducts investiture ceremonies for The Queen's Birthday Honours and the Order of Papua New Guinea, which recognise outstanding service rendered by members of the public in both the public and private sectors.

Papua New Guinea

Government House, Solomon Islands

The Solomon Islands is a Commonwealth realm made up of six major islands and over 900 smaller islands in the western Pacific Ocean, lying east of Papua New Guinea. The islands cover a land area of 11,000 square miles (28,489 square kilometres) and the population numbers over 500,000 people.

The Melanesian peoples have lived in the islands for thousands of years, and in 1568, the Spanish explorer, Álvaro de Mendaña was the first European to visit them, naming them the Islas Salomón. The British began to explore the area in the late 19th century, and in 1893, Captain Gibson RN declared the southern Solomon Islands as a British protectorate. The Solomon Islands gained self-government in 1976 and independence in 1978. The British monarch in the Solomon Islands was represented by Resident Commissioners and Governors of the Solomon Islands, who became known as Governors-General upon independence.

The settlement of Tulagi was the capital of the British Solomon Islands Protectorate from 1896 to 1942. The first of many Government Houses in the Solomon Islands was a traditional beach hut in Tulagi occupied by the Resident Commissioner, Charles Woodford, in 1897. A more substantial residence was built in 1898, overlooking Tulagi harbour, and this was replaced in 1905 by a larger house nearby, which served until 1933 when it succumbed to an infestation of white ants that destroyed it. The fourth Government House in Tulagi was built the same year and was occupied from 1934.

Above left and left: Government House in the Solomon Islands was previously a US army officers' quarters and a New Zealand military hospital during the Second World War.

Maxwell Banyo/Government House Solomon Islands

The first Government House in the new capital of Honiara (which was officially designated as the capital in 1952) was a former US army officers' quarters and also a New Zealand military hospital that was designated as an official residence following the Second World War. From 1952, Government House was the home of the High Commissioner for the Western Pacific, a role that was combined with that of the Governor of the Solomon Islands.

This single-storey house was adapted in 1967 with a new construction designed by Warren and Mahoney, architects from Christchurch, New Zealand, and the new building was completed in 1969. The grounds of Government House contain a traditional meeting place which has been used for investitures, receptions and official ceremonies by successive Governors-General. The traditional-style hut alongside the 'modern' buildings of Government House and the staff offices brings a sense of tradition to the grounds. The meeting hut was also created as a tribute to the early beginnings of Government House, echoing the simple hut first created at Tulagi, before the residence moved to Honiara.

Above and below: The grounds of Government House in Honiara contain a traditional-style meeting place, which has been used for investitures, receptions and official ceremonies by successive Governors-General.

Queen Elizabeth II first visited the Solomon Islands in 1974, accompanied by the Duke of Edinburgh, Princess Anne and Captain Mark Phillips. The Queen and Prince Philip returned there in 1982, following the Commonwealth Games in Australia. Prince Philip has also been to the Solomon Islands on solo visits in 1959 and 1971. The Duke and Duchess of Gloucester represented The Queen at the independence celebrations for the Solomon Islands in 1978. The Duke and Duchess of Cambridge also paid a visit in 2012 to celebrate The Queen's Diamond Jubilee with the islanders.

In 2019, the Prince of Wales was welcomed to the Solomon Islands for the first time when he went to a Service of Thanksgiving at St Barnabas Anglican Cathedral before attending meetings at Government House with the Governor-General, Sir David Vunagi. The Prince also laid a wreath at the Solomon Islands Scouts' and Coastwatchers' Memorial honouring Solomon Islanders during the Second World War, visited Parliament House in Honiara and promoted local climate change projects focused on protecting the world's oceans.

Maxwell Banyo/Government House Solomon Islands

Maxwell Banyo/Government House Solomon Islands

Solomon Islands

John Finch

Government House, St Lucia

The island of St Lucia is a sovereign nation in the eastern Caribbean, located north-west of the larger island of Barbados. It covers around 240 square miles (620 square kilometres) and has a population of over 165,000 people. The French were the island's first European settlers and they signed a treaty with the native Carib Indians in 1660. In 1664, Thomas Warner, the son of the Governor of St Kitts, settled in St Lucia on behalf of the English, but the French West India Company arrived two years later to claim the island and over the following 150 years, control of St Lucia changed between the French and the British a total of 14 times.

In 1814, St Lucia became established as a British settlement, although the French influence remained through the language, culture and legal practice, which was originally based on the Francophone system. St Lucia became independent in 1979 as a Commonwealth realm, with the monarch represented by the Governor-General. Previously, the British Crown had been represented by a series of Commissioners, Administrators and later Governors of St Lucia.

Government House is the official residence of the Governor-General of St Lucia, located on a hill known as Morne Fortune (literally 'Hill of Good Fortune'), near the capital of Castries. The first Government House built on the site was destroyed by a hurricane in 1817 before it was completed, and a second house was built there in 1819. The timber-framed house was abandoned in 1865 when it began to deteriorate, and the formal home was moved to a nearby military barracks.

Below: A St Lucian postage stamp dating from around 1938, featuring a portrait of King George VI against a background image of Government House.

Meister Photos/Shutterstock 1528469918

Above: The rear view of Government House in St Lucia shows the official residence's unique architectural styles.

Construction of the third and current Government House began in 1894 and it was completed a year later. The large brick-built house has stood the test of time, although constant repairs and renovations are required. The property is one of the few remaining Victorian buildings on the island and has the appearance of a large family residence, although the flag tower and royal coat of arms give it a regal air. The spacious official reception rooms feature a small dais with portraits of the monarch and other significant figures, and offer commanding views of Castries, the capital of St Lucia. Within Government House today is Le Pavillon Royal Museum, which features important historical artefacts, silverware, medals and awards, as well as original architectural drawings of the house.

Government House has welcomed many royal guests to St Lucia. Queen Elizabeth II first visited the island in 1966 with Prince Philip, Duke of Edinburgh, during her Caribbean tour on the Royal Yacht *Britannia*. The royal couple opened the Winban Research Centre, enjoyed traditional dancing and steel-band music, and watched a fireworks display over the harbour. Their visit is commemorated with a date reference on the gates of Government House. In 1985, The Queen and Prince Philip returned when they laid the foundation stone for the new headquarters of the St Lucia Red Cross and met young people undertaking the Duke of Edinburgh's Award Scheme on the island. Princess Alexandra represented The Queen during St Lucia's independence celebrations in 1979 and the Prince of Wales attended the 10th anniversary of independence in 1989. The Earl and Countess of Wessex visited the St Lucia School of Music in Castries in 2012, during their Diamond Jubilee tour on behalf of The Queen.

Below: The reception rooms at Government House feature large portraits of Queen Elizabeth II and former Governors-General. There are also fine views across the island from the wrap around verandah.

In 2016, Prince Harry travelled to St Lucia as part of his Caribbean tour when he unveiled St Lucia's dedication to 'The Queen's Commonwealth Canopy' at Castries Water Works Reserve and presented Duke of Edinburgh's Award certificates at Government House. In 2019, the Prince of Wales began his Caribbean tour in St Lucia when he visited the island to mark the country's 40th anniversary of independence and to attend a youth rally at Vieux Fort, although the Prince did not visit Government House on this occasion.

St Lucia

Phil Noble/PA Images/41884909

Government House, St Vincent and the Grenadines

St Vincent and the Grenadines is a Commonwealth realm in the eastern Caribbean in the southern chain of the Windward Islands. It comprises the main island of St Vincent as well as several smaller islands in the Grenadines covering a total of 150 square miles (390 square kilometres). St Vincent and the Grenadines is considered to be a densely populated country with over 100,000 residents. Similar to its neighbour St Lucia, the islands of St Vincent and the Grenadines were settled by the French initially in the 17th century, but there followed many years of both French and British administration as disputes were fought between the two colonial nations.

From the late 18th century, St Vincent and the Grenadines came under the British administration and from 1763 until its independence in 1979, the islands were administered under a succession of Lieutenant-Governors, Governors and Administrators representing the British Crown. The Governors of St Vincent and the Grenadines lived in several different official houses over the years. In 1791, records show that Government House was somewhere in the area of Calliaqua and that by the time of the Second Carib War in 1795–97, Government House was in Montrose. This property fell into disrepair and a new Government House was built in the capital, Kingstown, on what is now the site of an international bank. The location was chosen as it was close to the government offices in Kingstown.

In 1828, another Government House was built on 3-acres (1.2-hectares) of land in the Botanical Gardens, but this house also became rundown. The present-day Government House was built in 1886 on the same plot and is the official residence of the Governor-General of St Vincent and the Grenadines. Government House is located in Old Montrose, on the outskirts of Kingstown and is considered to be one of St Vincent's historic buildings.

Located north of Kingstown, the Botanical Gardens on St Vincent are regarded as one of the oldest botanical gardens in the Western Hemisphere. They feature lush, tropical gardens that are home to many plants, flowers, trees and birds. The Botanical Gardens were created in 1765 by the newly appointed Governor of the British Caribbean Islands, Colonel Robert Melville, and the military surgeon in St Vincent, George Young, on 6-acres

Above left: In 2019, the Prince of Wales visited the Botanical Gardens in St Vincent during a tour of the Caribbean.

Right: The Botanical Gardens on St Vincent are considered to be one of the oldest botanical gardens in the Western Hemisphere.

(2.4-hectares) of land that had previously been restricted to military use. The area was later expanded to 20-acres (8-hectares). The gardens were vital to the economic prosperity of the islands and many plants were imported from Kew Gardens in London. The Botanical Gardens are also famous for the visit of Captain William Bligh to the Caribbean in 1793 (his first voyage had resulted in the infamous mutiny on *The Bounty*). Bligh arrived with different plants from the South Pacific, including a breadfruit tree that he introduced to the island's gardens, whose fruit when roasted is one of the Caribbean's most popular dishes.

St Vincent and the Grenadines has hosted a number of royal guests. Queen Elizabeth II first visited the Commonwealth realm with Prince Philip, Duke of Edinburgh, in 1966 during a Caribbean tour, when they received an official welcome at Victoria Park in Kingstown, attended morning service at St George's Cathedral and visited the Colonial Hospital. In 1985, the royal couple returned to the islands to attend the Independence Anniversary Parade and Prince Philip also presented Duke of Edinburgh Gold Awards to young people during a ceremony at Government House.

However, The Queen wasn't the first royal visitor to St Vincent as her sister, Princess Margaret, had visited the island during an extensive royal tour of the Caribbean in 1955 on the Royal Yacht *Britannia*. The Princess came to fall in love with the Grenadines and in 1960, she was given a small piece of land on the southern tip of the tiny island of Mustique as a wedding present by her good friend, Colin Tennant, 3rd Baron Glenconner, who had purchased the island in 1958. A beautiful residence named 'Les Jolies Eaux' was built on the site and Princess Margaret would spend long holidays in Mustique during the British winter from the 1960s right through to the 1990s.

In 2012, the Earl and Countess of Wessex visited St Vincent and the Grenadines to mark The Queen's Diamond Jubilee when they planted a ceremonial tree and viewed the celebrations taking place in the islands. Prince Harry also went there in 2016, as part of his Caribbean tour of the region, during which he unveiled St Vincent's dedication to 'The Queen's Commonwealth Canopy' at the Vermont Nature Trail.

In 2019, the Prince of Wales and the Duchess of Cornwall travelled to St Vincent and the Grenadines, where they laid a wreath at the Cenotaph, visited a school and the cathedral, and spent time meeting local people. The Prince and the Duchess also attended a reception with the Governor-General at the Prime Minister's Residence in Kingstown.

St Vincent and the Grenadines

Government House, St Kitts and Government House, Nevis

St Kitts and Nevis, also known as St Christopher and Nevis, is an island realm in the north-west of the Caribbean region. It is one of the smallest sovereign states of the Americas, in both area and population. The larger island of St Kitts and the smaller island of Nevis cover an area of approximately 100 square miles (260 square kilometres) and have a population of around 60,000 people.

The islands were amongst the first to be settled by Europeans in the 16th and 17th centuries, and the French, Dutch, Spanish and British all fought for control of the various islands of the north-west Caribbean. In 1713, the French relinquished control of St Kitts and Nevis to the British. By the early 19th century, St Kitts was one of the richest British settlements in the Caribbean by its size, largely as a result of the international sugar trade that was fuelled by the slavery and transportation of people from Africa to work on plantations.

St Kitts and Nevis were joined together with nearby Anguilla as an associated state of the United Kingdom in 1967, but Anguilla separated in 1977 to administer its own affairs as a British Overseas Territory. St Kitts and Nevis became an independent nation in 1983. Today, the country is a Commonwealth realm with Queen Elizabeth II as the head of state, represented by the Governor-General of the Federation of St Kitts and Nevis.

Government House in Basseterre, the capital of St Kitts and Nevis, is the official Vice-Regal residence of the Governor-General. The two-storey building is also known as Springfield House and the original property was built around 1834. In around 1837, the 25-acre (10-hectare) estate, then part of the Diamond Estate, was sold by Sir Henry Blake to Thomas Harper, who began to renovate a large house named Springfield. Debts forced the property to pass on to Robert Sharry Harper as part of his marriage settlement to Mary Amory.

With the establishment of the Diocese of Antigua and the archdeaconry of St Kitts in 1842, the new Archdeacon Francis Robert Braithwaite bought the Springfield estate from the Harpers in 1848 to use as an ecclesiastical residence. Braithwaite attracted attention when he was involved in a rumoured local scandal by seducing a young woman and refusing to marry her, resulting in her premature death.

Image: St Kitts and Nevis Information Service

St Kitts and Nevis

Above: Government House in Basseterre, on the island of St Kitts is a two-storey house built in around 1834 that is also known as Springfield House.

In 1855, it was declared that Springfield House could also be used for public purposes, such as the meetings of the Governor, the Privy Council or the Assembly. However, the property continued to be utilised by the church and it became the residence of the Rector of St George, the Venerable Archdeacon Jermyn in 1856. It remained this way until the disestablishment of the church in 1874, and when Archdeacon Gibbs retired in 1882, Springfield House became available for use by the island's official administration.

The house was in great disrepair and after much renovation work, it was designated as an official residence albeit for the head of government rather than as a Vice-Regal residence. The role of the head of government had evolved over time in St Kitts to carry the title of the President of St Christopher, Nevis and Anguilla, jointly based in St Kitts. This role changed from President to Commissioner to Administrator during the 20th century.

During the late 19th century, Springfield House featured ground-floor reception rooms, including a large drawing room and dining room with five guest bedrooms upstairs. Some furniture was brought from previous temporary Government Houses on the island, but the new residents were advised to bring their own linen and cutlery with them, and they were expected to pay for candles and oil at their own expense.

Springfield House was sometimes referred to as Government House during the late 19th century although, rather confusingly, another house in the area at Victoria Road was also known as Government House and was used by the Vice-Regal representative. There was an overlap in the role of both properties. The use of Government House on Victoria Road as an official residence came to an end during the Second World War and in 1946, the house became part of the St Kitts Girl's High School and later the western campus of Basseterre High School.

From 1946, Springfield House on St Kitts became the official residence of the Vice-Regal representative on the island, the Governor-General of St Kitts, and it was formally named Government House. Renovation works were undertaken in 2004 when a large dining room was added, and the offices of the Governor-General were refurbished.

St Kitts and Nevis

Left: Government House on the island of Nevis was built in 1909 as the Vice-Regal residence for the Governor. The large two-storey property in Charlestown was recently restored after being damaged by a hurricane.

Queen Elizabeth II and the Duke of Edinburgh first visited St Kitts and Nevis in 1966, when they attended an investiture ceremony at Government House on St Kitts and The Queen also planted a tree at Nevis Grammar School. The royal couple returned to the islands in 1985, when they held a reception on-board the Royal Yacht *Britannia*.

The Queen's sister, Princess Margaret, represented the sovereign in 1983 at the independence ceremonies held for St Kitts and Nevis. In 2012, to celebrate the Queen's Diamond Jubilee, the Earl and Countess of Wessex were welcomed to St Kitts and Nevis and spent time at the Basseterre National Park.

Prince Harry visited the islands in 2016 during his Caribbean tour, when he unveiled St Kitts and Nevis' contribution to the global environmental project known as 'The Queen's Commonwealth Canopy' at the Central Forest Reserve National Park. He was also invited to a sea turtle conservation project on the island of Nevis.

A second Government House can also be found on the smaller island of Nevis. Built in 1909 as the Vice-Regal residence for Nevis, the large two-storey building in Charlestown was recently restored after it became a ruin and was uninhabitable following extensive hurricane damage. A renovation project by the Nevis Island Administration took place to restore the former residence for official use by the Deputy Governor-General of St Kitts and Nevis (also the Vice-Regal representative on Nevis Island) and as a local history museum.

The Prince of Wales and the Duchess of Cornwall visited Government House in Nevis during their Caribbean tour in 2019 and attended a reception in the grounds given by the Deputy Governor-General. The royal couple also travelled to St Kitts where they visited the National Museum and attended a reception at Government House in Basseterre hosted by the Governor-General.

St Kitts and Nevis

Michael Coghlan

Michael Coghlan

Government House, Tuvalu

Tuvalu is a remote island nation in the Pacific Ocean, roughly midway between Australia and Hawaii. The three reef islands and six atolls cover 10 square miles (26 square kilometres) and have a population of around 11,500 people.

The indigenous peoples of the archipelago were Polynesians before the arrival of European settlers in the 1800s. In 1892, the islands, then known as the Ellice Islands, were joined with a nearby island group to form the Gilbert and Ellice Islands. They were administered as a British protectorate by a Resident Commissioner from 1892 to 1976.

The Gilbert and Ellice Islands separated in 1975–76, with the Gilbert Islands becoming the Republic of Kiribati and the Ellice Islands becoming the Commonwealth realm of Tuvalu, later gaining full independence in 1978.

The monarchy in Tuvalu was represented first by the Resident Commissioner and today by the Governor-General of Tuvalu. Several houses have been occupied over time as Government House by the Vice-Regal representatives.

Due to its remote location in the Pacific Ocean, royal guests in Tuvalu have been rare. Queen Elizabeth II and the Duke of Edinburgh visited Tuvalu for the only time in September 1982 as part of a month-long tour of the Pacific, when the royal couple were famously carried onto the island in canoes borne aloft by local people. The Queen and Prince Philip attended a feast in their honour and watched indigenous dancing and sports, as well as visiting the local hospital, school and laying the foundation stone for the new Parliament buildings.

Princess Margaret represented The Queen at Tuvalu's independence ceremonies in 1978, although it was reported at the time that her visit had to be cut short as she was suffering from a temperature of 104°F (40°C) and had to be flown to Sydney for treatment in a New Zealand Air Forces plane. The local hospital that she had been due to visit was opened in her name as The Princess Margaret Hospital in Funafuti, which continues to serve the islands' residents today.

Above: Government House in Tuvalu is a single-storey building. Little is known about its origins.

In 2012, the Duke and Duchess of Cambridge went to Tuvalu as part of a Pacific tour to mark The Queen's Diamond Jubilee, during which they toured a primary school and university campus, and watched demonstrations of island crafts and cooking. The royal couple were photographed wearing colourful Pacific-island shirts and grass skirts to join in with the traditional dancing.

Tuvalu

Crown Dependencies

The Crown Dependencies are independently administered jurisdictions of the British Crown that do not form part of the United Kingdom or the British Overseas Territories. Each of the Crown Dependencies are defined uniquely and are considered self-governing, although it is argued that the United Kingdom has the authority to pass some legislation affecting the Crown Dependencies, particularly in relation to defence and foreign affairs.

Internationally, the Crown Dependencies are not deemed to be sovereign states, so they are not individual members of the Commonwealth, although they all have independent Legislatures who legislate on local matters and thus they are members of the Commonwealth Parliamentary Association, for example, in their own right. The Crown Dependencies also participate independently in the Commonwealth Games and many other Commonwealth organisations in their own right.

The monarch has a unique and independent relationship with the Crown Dependencies and is represented by a Lieutenant-Governor, who usually resides at Government House. The role of Lieutenant-Governor is largely ceremonial and charitable today and involves carrying out duties on behalf of the monarch, such as awarding honours and medals, hosting royal visits and celebrating citizens' achievements, including when they reach their 100th birthdays. The three Crown Dependencies are the Bailiwick of Jersey and the Bailiwick of Guernsey in the English Channel, and the Isle of Man in the Irish Sea.

In the two Bailiwicks of Guernsey and Jersey, more commonly known as the Channel Islands, the monarch is popularly referred to as the Duke of Normandy. This is as a result of the Islands being annexed by the Duchy of Normandy from the Duchy of Brittany in AD 933. The Duke of Normandy became one of the hereditary titles of the monarchs of England following the Norman conquest under William the Conqueror, Duke of Normandy, who claimed the title King of England in 1066.

In the Isle of Man, the British monarch is known as the Lord of Mann, a title held by Norse, Scottish and English kings and nobles until it was adopted by the British monarch in 1765.

Crown Dependencies

Government House, Jersey

Jersey is the largest of the Channel Islands at just over 45 square miles (116 square kilometres) in the English Channel between France and England. A Crown Dependency, Jersey has been of strategic and logistical importance for many years, and it is a self-governing parliamentary democracy under the British Crown, with its own financial, legal and judicial systems.

The history of Jersey has been influenced by its strategic location in the English Channel off the coast of northern France, although there is evidence of Bronze Age and Iron Age settlements on the island. Jersey came under the jurisdiction of the Dukes of Normandy in AD 933 and passed to the English Crown in 1066 under William the Conqueror, Duke of Normandy. It has been a Crown Dependency ever since.

The Lieutenant-Governor on the island is the personal representative of the monarch. The official residence of the Lieutenant-Governor of Jersey is Government House, a large, comfortable property with views across Jersey's capital St Helier. It is also used for ceremonial events, receptions and meetings with foreign dignitaries, as well as hosting visits by the monarch, known as the Duke of Normandy in Jersey, or members of the Royal Family.

The current Government House is at least the fifth official residence of the Governors and later the Lieutenant-Governors of Jersey. Early Governors of the island lived at the famous Mont Orgueil, also known as Gorey Castle, which has been in existence since 1204.

Later, Governors of Jersey resided at Elizabeth Castle, situated on a small rocky outcrop just outside the port of

Left: The main entrance gates to Government House in Jersey on St Saviour's Hill.

Right: The current Government House in Jersey is located on a hill in the parish of St Saviour, a short distance from the centre of the capital, St Helier. The original two-storey villa was built in around 1814 by a local ship owner, Francis Janvrin and it was originally named 'Belmont'.

Jeffrey Hyland

St Helier, although being a tidal island, the castle wasn't always a convenient official home and Governors lived at various houses in the capital before the present Government House was adopted.

Today, Government House on Jersey is located on a hill in the parish of St Saviour, a short distance from the centre of St Helier. In 1803, Reverend Philip Le Breton, Rector of the local St Saviour's Church, bought the land on which the current residence is situated, to build a family home. The property was then bought by a local ship owner, Francis Janvrin, in 1814, who demolished it and built a two-storey villa, calling the house, Belmont. It is thanks to Janvrin that the house contains a number of features made of acajou mahogany, in particular the imposing main staircase, which remains today. The dark wood used throughout the building was brought from South America on Janvrin's ships in the early 19th century.

In 1822, the Lieutenant-Governor Major General Sir Colin Halkett purchased Belmont as the new Government House because he was unhappy with his residence in King Street in the centre of town. He thought that the Lieutenant-Governor *"would at Belmont possess the desirable opportunity of seeing together, without apparent partiality, such of the inhabitants, and strangers, as naturally expected to be invited to Government House."*

Improvements and extensions to the house were made in the second half of the 19th century, such as the addition of a third storey to the main house and the construction of a gatehouse and various outbuildings including a stable block, which is now divided into cottages and offices. The symmetrical lines of the early 19th-century villa were altered and the present porte cochère entrance was also added, giving the residence a regal but asymmetrical style.

The interior of Jersey's Government House is dominated by the South American mahogany main staircase and the style is of a late 19th-century villa, although architrave features inside the house date from the Regency period when it was constructed. Three marble fireplaces in the ground-floor reception rooms depict different classical themes and replace earlier wooden overmantels. The present kitchens were added in 1936 by local Jersey contractor, Charles Le Quesne Ltd in place of the previous extensive kitchens in the basement. The top storey of the residence was used as staff quarters.

Jersey

During the Second World War, the Channel Islands were occupied by the German Army and Government House in Jersey was seized by the German General Graf von Schmettow, who lived there as Commandant of the Island. The Government House butler and his wife remained throughout the war years and it was largely due to them that the property remained intact.

The imposing driveway to Government House was previously a public lane to the nearby St Saviour's Church. It was bought in 1810 on the condition that it was not closed to the public until the new military road (now St Saviour's Hill) was completed. The 12-acre (5-hectare) grounds include a variety of landscapes, gardens and features, such as a formal garden, a woodland valley, a walled kitchen garden and ornamental lake and fountain.

The grounds also contain many of the oldest trees on the island, as during the German occupation between July 1940 and May 1945, most trees across the island were cut down for fuel. However, as Government House had been requisitioned, the trees in its grounds were preserved on the orders of the German Commandant.

The Lieutenant-Governor of Jersey holds large receptions and garden parties in the grounds of Government House and there are many trees planted by royal visitors and numerous commemorative monuments. The 13-metre wooden flagpole flies the Lieutenant-Governor's flag when he or she is in residence.

The estate has four cannons on the ramparts overlooking the town. The cannons were made in the early 19th century and are naval 64-pounder muzzle-loaders converted from 8-inch smooth bore to rifled barrels.

Today, Government House welcomes over 3,000 guests and visitors to functions each year and it remains the official residence of the Lieutenant-Governor of Jersey and their family. Royalty and other important dignitaries stay there during their visits to Jersey and Queen Elizabeth II, as Duke of Normandy, has visited Government House many times. The Queen's first visit to Jersey was in 1949 when she was Princess Elizabeth. The last time that The Queen was welcomed to Government House was in 2005 for the 60th anniversary of the Liberation of Jersey.

Left: A granite seat in the grounds of Government House in Jersey commemorates the Diamond Wedding Anniversary of Queen Elizabeth II and Prince Philip, Duke of Edinburgh, and the 90th anniversary of the Battle of Cambrai on 20 November 2007. The First World War battle in Northern France was especially significant to local people in Jersey as many soldiers who fought and died there came from the local area.

Jersey

All images: Courtesy of Government House, Guernsey

Government House, Guernsey

Located in the Channel Islands, Guernsey is a 25 square mile (65 square kilometre) island in the English Channel, off the coast of Normandy in France. A British Crown Dependency, Guernsey is the largest island in the administrative jurisdiction of the Bailiwick of Guernsey, which comprises the islands of Guernsey, Sark, Alderney, Brecqhou, Herm, Jethou and Lihou.

The history of the Bailiwick of Guernsey dates from AD 933, when the Channel Islands came under the jurisdiction of the Duchy of Normandy, which in turn became part of the English Crown in 1066 under William the Conqueror.

When Normandy separated from the English Crown in 1204, the Channel Islands remained a Crown Dependency. During the English Civil War in the 1640s, Guernsey sided with the Parliamentarians, while Jersey remained Royalist. Like its neighbour Jersey, the islands of the Bailiwick of Guernsey were occupied by the German Army during the Second World War.

The Bailiwick of Guernsey is headed by a Bailiff and it has its own Legislature, with a Lieutenant-Governor representing the Crown. As the official residence of the Lieutenant-Governor of Guernsey, Government House is located a short drive from the centre of the capital, St Peter Port.

A large, Georgian three-storey, whitewashed central residence with two additional wings of the property, Government House has the feel of a sizable country home without being too grand.

The current Government House is the latest in a long line of previous residences that have been the official home of the Lieutenant-Governors of Guernsey, including the most famous, Old Government House, which is now a luxury five-star hotel in the centre of St Peter Port.

Guernsey

Originally known as 'Le Mont', the present-day Government House has been the home of the monarch's representative on the island twice in its history. It was built by Nicolas Maingy as an elegant Georgian mansion and was first inhabited by Major-General John Small, the Lieutenant-Governor of Guernsey from 1793 to 1796. The property reverted to private ownership belonging to a succession of Guernsey's wealthiest residents.

The Mount, as it was known, became the current Government House again in 1925, when it was purchased by the Crown and it has been the residence of the Lieutenant-Governor of Guernsey ever since, except for the period during the Second World War when it was occupied by the German Army Commandant.

The interior of the house has a number of official reception rooms, including a grand dining room with a table that can accommodate 16 people at formal dinners. The comfortable ballroom is used for receptions and features a grand piano displaying photographs of the monarch and members of the Royal Family who have stayed at Government House. The

Above: The dining room at Government House has a grand dining table that can accommodate 16 people at formal dinners.

All images: Courtesy of Government House, Guernsey

Left: The Georgian property at Government House in Guernsey is made up of a central building with two wings.

All images: Courtesy of Government House, Guernsey

Above: The ballroom is used for receptions and small ceremonial events with the Lieutenant-Governor of Guernsey.

official rooms also feature several portraits of former Lieutenant-Governors and other people who have played a significant part in Guernsey's history.

The grounds of Government House comprise 10-acres (4-hectares) of parkland and landscaped gardens featuring many mature trees, including two trees planted by Queen Elizabeth II during her visits to Guernsey in 1989 and 2001, as well as trees planted by other royal and distinguished visitors.

The grounds also contain a specialist camellia collection and a historic Victorian walled garden that covers over 1,700 square metres. One of the best examples of a traditional walled garden in the British Isles, it is used to provide the residence with hundreds of different types of fruit, vegetables and cut flowers.

Many official visitors to Guernsey are welcomed at Government House and a wide range of public functions, from charity receptions and official dinners to school sports days, are held in its house and grounds.

The first royal visit to Guernsey by a reigning monarch took place on 23 August 1846, when Queen Victoria and Prince Albert arrived in St Peter Port on the Royal Yacht *Victoria and Albert*.

Queen Elizabeth II first went to Guernsey as Princess Elizabeth with her husband, the Duke of Edinburgh, during a tour of the Channel Islands in June 1949. The Princess opened the new Princess Elizabeth Hospital in Guernsey with a silver key and the royal couple had dinner at the Old Government House Hotel, before departing later that evening on HMS *Anson*.

The Queen's first visit to Guernsey after she become monarch was in July 1957, when the royal couple were greeted by over 6,000 school children gathered to welcome them. The Queen has returned in 1978, 1989, 2001 and most recently in 2005, when the royal couple commemorated the 60th anniversary of the liberation of the island from German occupation during the Second World War.

Over the years, many members of the Royal Family have visited Guernsey. In July 2012, the Prince of Wales and the Duchess of Cornwall visited the Bailiwick of Guernsey as part of their tour of the Channel Islands to celebrate The Queen's Diamond Jubilee. During their visit, the royal couple met the patients and staff of a local hospice, as well as meeting local politicians and attending a youth event involving 400 local children.

Guernsey

Island Hall, Alderney

Alderney is the most northerly of the inhabited Channel Islands and is part of the Bailiwick of Guernsey, a Crown Dependency. The island is about 3 miles long by 1½ miles wide (5 kilometres long by 2.4 kilometres wide) and is geographically the closest of the Channel Islands to both the French and English coastlines. It has a small population of around 2,000 permanent residents.

Alderney shares its history with the other Channel Islands in that it became part of the Duchy of Normandy in AD 933. After a period of time under the control of the Abbey of Mont Saint-Michel and the Bishop of Coutances, Alderney sided with the English monarch in 1204, along with the rest of the Channel Islands. During the English Civil Wars in the 1640s, Alderney was held by a parliamentary garrison under the Lieutenant-Governor, Nicholas Ling. The governorship of Alderney passed through several families over the next centuries, including the de Carterets family of Jersey followed by the Andros of Guernsey and then the Le Mesurier family of Guernsey, which lasted until 1825.

The Le Mesurier family grew wealthy from privateering (engaging in maritime warfare under a commission of war) and the island's capital of St Anne was established. Island Hall was built in around 1763 by Governor John Le Mesurier and served as Alderney's equivalent of Government House, then later as a Catholic convent school. The Alderney Court House was built around the same time in 1770 and both were established as the seats of government and official life on the island. In 1825, the last of the hereditary Governors of Alderney, another John Le Mesurier, relinquished his role and following this, the States of

Below: The Island Hall in Alderney has held many official and royal functions in the absence of a Government House and the island's official flagpole is located in its grounds.

Neil Howard

Right: Victoria Street in Alderney was renamed to commemorate the visit of Queen Victoria and Prince Albert in 1854.

Neil Howard

Alderney was established as the governmental and legislative body of the island, headed by a President.

The link with the Crown, however, continued as today Alderney is part of the Bailiwick of Guernsey and as such the Crown is represented through the Lieutenant-Governor of Guernsey. Island Hall remains as one of the official buildings of the island, along with the Alderney Court House, and today it functions as the island's main library and museum but sometimes official functions are held there and the island's official flagpole is located in its grounds.

The Royal Family has long kept a close interest in the Crown Dependencies in the Channel Islands. Queen Victoria and Prince Albert visited Alderney on 9 August 1854, the first of three occasions that The Queen would go to the island. Her visit is commemorated in the renaming of the main high street from Rue Grosnez to Victoria Street. The nearby Royal Connaught Square is also said to be named after The Queen's third son, Prince Arthur, Duke of Connaught, who visited Alderney with Queen Victoria on one of her subsequent trips.

In recent years, Queen Elizabeth II and members of the Royal Family have visited Alderney several times. The Queen first went there in June 1949 when, as Princess Elizabeth, she toured the Channel Islands with the Duke of Edinburgh. The Queen and Prince Philip returned to Alderney in 1978 and 1989, when they attended an official reception at Alderney's Island Hall. They also visited the island again in 2001. Island Hall also features a unique portrait of The Queen, one of four painted by artist June Mendoza in 1987 for different institutions.

In 2012, the Prince of Wales and Duchess of Cornwall arrived in Alderney by helicopter, on the final stop of their tour of the Bailiwick of Guernsey to mark The Queen's Diamond Jubilee. The royal couple travelled to Island Hall by vintage car where they viewed an exhibition of paintings by local children, before planting a royal oak tree.

Alderney

La Seigneurie, Sark

Sue Daly

Left: La Seigneurie in Sark has welcomed many members of the Royal Family over the years on visits to the historic residence and its beautiful gardens. The property is often open to the public and tourists visiting the tiny island.

The small island of Sark, with a population of about 600 people and an area of only 2 square miles (5 square kilometres), is part of the Bailiwick of Guernsey and as such the Crown is represented through the Lieutenant-Governor of Guernsey. Therefore, Sark doesn't have a Government House. However, Sark is in the unique position of being presided over by a hereditary Seigneur (or Lord of the Manor) and has an official residence – La Seigneurie.

Formerly the site of a 6th-century priory, the main house today dates from 1675 and has been home to two of Sark's three Seigneurial families: the Le Pelleys (from 1730) and the Collings (from 1852), ancestors of Seigneur Michael Beaumont who died in 2016. The building has been added to many times over the years and it is said to be modelled on the 'Jersey' design of four windows downstairs and five above using Jersey stone, which was very fashionable in the 18th and 19th centuries. There are said to be two ways to nearly every room in the main residence and 16 different staircases.

Notable features in the grounds of La Seigneurie include a 19th-century *colombier* (dove-cote), a small chapel and a signalling tower. Ownership of the *columbier* was an exclusive right of the Seigneur dating back centuries, when pigeons and doves were bred for food and to keep the number of birds under control to protect tenants' crops. The signalling tower dates from the Napoleonic Wars and was used for communicating with Guernsey on a clear day.

In recent years, Queen Elizabeth II and members of the Royal Family have visited Sark and have met the Seigneur of Sark and local people at La Seigneurie. The island is one of the few remaining places in the world where cars are banned from the roads and only tractors and horse-drawn vehicles are allowed and there has been no exception for The Queen. The Queen's first visit there was in 1949 as Princess Elizabeth with the Duke of Edinburgh, and she returned in 1978 following her Silver Jubilee and again in 1989 and 2001. Several members of the Royal Family have also visited Sark including Queen Elizabeth the Queen Mother, the Prince of Wales and the Duchess of Cornwall, and the Princess Royal.

Although the family of the Seigneur don't live full-time at the residence today, it is often open to the public as a local tourist attraction.

Sark

Government House, Isle of Man

The Isle of Man is a self-governing British Crown Dependency of 221 square miles (572 square kilometres) located in the Irish Sea between the islands of Great Britain and Ireland. The Isle of Man Parliament, Tynwald, is considered by many to be the oldest Parliament in the world at over 1,000 years old. The island has been inhabited since before 6500 BC with Gaelic, Norse and English influences in evidence. After a period of alternating rule by the Kings of Scotland and England, the island came under the feudal lordship of the English Crown in 1399.

As a Crown Dependency, the Isle of Man is presided over by a Lieutenant-Governor who represents the monarch. The sovereign in turn is known on the island as the Lord of Mann. The official residence of the Lieutenant-Governor is Government House, situated on Governor's Road in Onchan.

Used extensively for official functions and for important visitors to the Isle of Man, the current Government House was not the original residence on the island. Previous formal dwellings used over many hundreds of years included the medieval fortress of Castle Rushen, the grand residence of Lorne House in Castletown, the site of the stately Castle Mona Hotel, and the mansion known as Villa Marina.

The current Government House in the Isle of Man was originally called Bemahague Farm and was owned by the Heywood family. No traces of the original farm, which dated from the 16th century, remain, however the main part of the present residence was built between 1820 and 1830.

The first Lieutenant-Governor to live at there was Henry Brougham Loch, who held the position from 1863 to 1882 when the house was leased by the government. Further extensions to add to the accommodation for both guests and the servants at the house were made, which increased the property to its present size in 1904 when the Isle of Man government bought the house as a permanent official residence.

Above right: Government House in the Isle of Man was purchased by the Isle of Man Government in 1904 as a permanent official residence. It was previously known as Bemahague Farm and the current residence was built between 1820 and 1830.

Isle of Man

The house survived a major fire in the servants' quarters in 1914, which fortunately resulted in no loss of life or injuries. The opportunity to rebuild the oldest part of the building that was destroyed in the fire was later realised. In the late 1920s, Lady Frances Hill, wife of Lieutenant-Governor, Sir Claude Hill, was responsible for major decoration in the official rooms and installed decorative chandeliers from Paris.

During the Second World War, the residents of Government House on the Isle of Man were the Lieutenant-Governor, Vice-Admiral William Spencer Leveson-Gower, 4th Earl Granville, and his wife, Lady Rose Leveson-Gower. Lady Rose was an elder sister of Queen Elizabeth (later the Queen Mother). The Leveson-Gowers hosted King George VI and Queen Elizabeth at Government House during their time in residence and, in preparation for the royal visit, Lady Rose herself worked on the embroidered bedspread and satin hangings featuring the Royal Coat of Arms, which are still on display in the residence today. The Leverson-Gowers would go on to live at another Government House in Northern Ireland that is today known as Hillsborough Castle.

Another piece of wartime history can be seen in the hallway of Government House in the form of the brass bell of the ship, HMS *Manxman*, a minelayer that served with the Royal Navy during the Second World War. The ship paid numerous visits to the Isle of Man and many of its naval personnel were Manx residents.

Today, Government House has five main bedrooms, two large reception rooms and a wing of offices. A large portrait of King George III hangs in the dining room, which is a studio copy of the original by the Scottish artist Allan Ramsay that is part of the Royal Collection and hangs in Buckingham Palace. Numerous copies of the painting were made in the 1760s for distribution to Government Houses, and so the portrait at Government House on the

Below: The exterior of Government House in the Isle of Man has changed little since it was first built between 1820 and 1830.

Diane Kelsey/Government House Isle of Man

Isle of Man could have been sent to Governor John Murray in 1765, who was the first Governor to be directly appointed by the Crown.

One of the most unusual pieces in the house is a large silver casket containing an address to Major-General Sir William Fry, Lieutenant-Governor from 1919–1926, which was presented by the Tynwald, the Legislature of the Isle of Man. The casket was left to the house by the Fry family and it takes pride of place as a table decoration in the dining room. The casket is made of silver on an ebony base and contains panels with views of Government House, the Government Buildings, Tynwald Hill and Castle Rushen, together with the Manx coat-of-arms. The casket is topped with a model of a beautiful ship in honour of the maritime ancestors of the Isle of Man.

The grounds of Government House cover approximately 30-acres (12-hectares) and feature many exotic species of trees alongside plants native to the island.

Queen Elizabeth II and members of the Royal Family have been frequent visitors to the Isle of Man over the years though visits to Government House have been rare. The Queen and the Duke of Edinburgh's first official royal visit to the Isle of Man was in August 1955 when they arrived in the capital, Douglas on the Royal Yacht *Britannia*. During their visit to the island, the royal couple visited Rushen Castle and the town of Peel. Several of The Queen's visits to the Isle of Man have coincided with Tynwald Day, the island's national day usually observed on 5 July, when the monarch has presided over the official ceremonies to mark the annual event.

In 2012, the Prince of Wales and the Duchess of Cornwall were welcomed by large crowds on the Isle of Man when they visited to mark The Queen's Diamond Jubilee. The royal couple visited the National Sports Centre in Douglas before meeting members of the Peel lifeboat crew.

In 2018, the Duke of Cambridge visited the Isle of Man to watch the final stages of the Supersport TT Race, one of the most famous motorcycle races in the world.

The most recent royal visit was in 2019 when the Princess Royal visited the Isle of Man to open the newly renovated Market Hall before travelling to Ramsey Park Hotel, where she opened the hotel's new extension. The Princess then opened Peel Harbour Bridge and, in her role as Patron of the Cathedral Isle of Man's Development Appeal, visited the garden restorations.

Today, Government House on the Isle of Man has been designated a building of special architectural or historic interest by the Manx government in order to protect it for future generations.

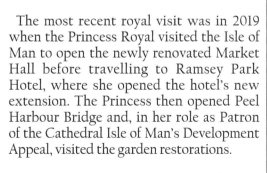

Right: The Lieutenant-Governor's official standard flying at Government House in the Isle of Man.

Isle of Man

Diane Kelsey/Government House Isle of Man

British Overseas Territories

The British Overseas Territories (BOT), which are sometimes known as the United Kingdom's Overseas Territories (UKOT), are a group of territories under the jurisdiction and sovereignty of the United Kingdom, although they are internally self-governing with their own elected Legislatures and currency. They all have their own identities and are represented by their own teams at the Commonwealth Games, although they are not currently independent members of the Commonwealth.

The United Kingdom retains responsibility for defence and foreign relations, and a number of British Overseas Territories are either uninhabited or have a transitory population of military or scientific personnel. All of the British Overseas Territories recognise the British monarch as their head of state and the Crown is represented locally by Governors (or in some cases by Commissioners, Administrators or Residents) in each territory.

There are currently 14 British Overseas Territories, of which nine have a current Government House. Those that don't have an official residence are: the British Indian Ocean Territory (a largely uninhabited group of small islands); the British Antarctic Territory, managed from the UK Foreign Office in London and only inhabited by scientists for part of the year; the Pitcairn Group of Islands in the Pacific Ocean, settled by the survivors of the mutiny on the HMS *Bounty* and one of the smallest

settled territories with just over 50 inhabitants – administered from the British High Commission in Wellington, New Zealand; and the Sovereign Base Areas in Cyprus (Akrotiri and Dhekelia), which are military bases run by the Sovereign Base Administration in conjunction with the Ministry of Defence and the British High Commission in Nicosia.

British Overseas Territories

Government House, Anguilla

David Jones

Anguilla is a small British Overseas Territory in the Caribbean, one of the most northerly of the Leeward Islands in the Lesser Antilles. The main 35 square mile (91 square kilometre) island is home to just under 15,000 people. Together with a number of little uninhabited islands, Anguilla lies in the hurricane belt of the western Atlantic Ocean and has faced frequent adversity, with the most recent major hurricane in September 2017 that caused much devastation.

Above: The Governor of Anguilla's official residence is Government House at Old Ta.

Anguilla was first settled by immigrants from South America, with the earliest settlements believed to be from around 1300. The date of the arrival of the first Europeans is disputed although the Dutch were said to have established a fort on the island in 1631. Anguilla was first settled by the British in 1650, who arrived from nearby settlements in St Kitts and Antigua. The island was administered from St Kitts until the 1960s, when an attempt to join it formally with the dependency of St Kitts and Nevis faced local opposition, as islanders wished to remain part of the United Kingdom. In 1980, Anguilla became a British Overseas Territory.

The Governor of Anguilla is the representative of the British monarch and appoints the Chief Minister. The Governor's official residence is Government House at Old Ta. Little is known about the modern Government House in Anguilla except that it was first built in 1969 and was substantially modernised in 1974. The property is the location for the island's formal ceremonies, such as investitures, citizenship ceremonies and the swearing-in of Government officials, as well as charity receptions and garden parties. In 2019, it was announced that Government House would be reconstructed in the same location due to ongoing structural damage caused by successive hurricanes.

Royal visits to Anguilla have been rare, with Queen Elizabeth II and Prince Philip visiting only once when they arrived on 18 February 1994 for a short two-day stay as part of a wider Caribbean tour. In 2012, the Earl and Countess of Wessex represented The Queen on a trip to Anguilla as part of a Diamond Jubilee tour of the region, during which they undertook many official engagements on the island and visited Government House.

Anguilla

Government House, Bermuda

Bermuda is a small 20 square mile (53 square kilometre) British Overseas Territory in the North Atlantic Ocean with a population of just over 71,000 people. It is a self-governing territory, with its own constitution, government and legislature.

Spanish explorers were first thought to have discovered Bermuda in the early 1500s, although the island archipelago was not permanently settled until around 1609, when the English Virginia Company, who had established Jamestown in the Americas, landed on the islands. The English Crown took over the administration in 1684, although Governors of Bermuda had been appointed since around 1612, at the same time as St George's was established as the first capital of the territory. In 1790, the government of Bermuda set aside about 145-acres (59-hectares) for a future capital to be named after Governor Henry Hamilton, and the island's capital moved to Hamilton from St George's in 1815.

Government House is the official residence of the Governor of Bermuda, the representative of the British monarch on the island. The property is located on Langton Hill, overlooking the North Shore in Hamilton. The house and grounds are one of the largest Government Houses in the Commonwealth. The present building replaced an earlier house that had served as the official residence from 1815 and was called 'Mount Langton', which had been named after a Scottish estate belonging to Sir James Cockburn, Governor of Bermuda from 1814 to 1816.

Constructed in the Italianate style, Government House was designed by Scottish architect William Hay, whose best-known project in Bermuda was the impressive Anglican cathedral in Hamilton. After Hay's death in 1888, two Bermudians, William Cardy Hallet, the Colonial Surveyor, and the master carpenter, John Henry Jackson, were brought in to finish the new residence, which was completed in 1892.

Built with stone said to be imported from France, Government House in Bermuda is an imposing property visible from afar with its stone towers and arches. The main residence

Lucy Pickles

Bermuda

has more than 30 rooms, including a large drawing room and dining room for formal entertaining, which open onto a sun terrace overlooking the swimming pool, tennis courts and garden. The upstairs features a large Royal Suite, the private rooms of the Governor and four guest bedrooms which have stunning views across Hamilton's harbour.

The house contains fine artworks of Bermudan heritage, many on loan from the United Kingdom Government Collection and from local museums. A wooden chest in the hallway dates from around 1740 and is one of the oldest pieces of Bermudan furniture in the residence. Other items on permanent loan from the Bermuda National Trust include three Sévres porcelain vases. Signed portrait photographs of the many royal visitors to the house are found in the main drawing room, including one of the present Duchess of Gloucester, who is a regular visitor to Bermuda as the Colonel-in-Chief of the Royal Bermuda Regiment. Two 1953 Coronation chairs can be found in Government House that were given by a former Governor, Sir Edwin Leather, in the 1970s. He also donated a unique piece of masonry from the British Houses of Parliament that had been found amongst the rubble in 1941 when the main chamber was bombed during the Second World War, and this is now displayed in the gardens of Government House.

The large grounds extend to 33-acres (13.4-hectares) and are one of the largest open spaces in Bermuda, containing many unique local species including cedars and spice trees. Many trees in the grounds were planted by Queen Elizabeth II, members of the Royal Family and other distinguished visitors such as Winston Churchill and Emperor Haile Selassie of Ethiopia. One of the earliest royal guests was King George V (when he was a young Prince George of Wales), who planted a tree at Government House during his visit to Bermuda as a midshipman in the Royal Navy in the early 1880s. Outside the main entrance to the house are three historic cannons, which have been in their present position since 1919.

The grounds were closed to the public in 1973, although many Bermudans still attend public events at Government House throughout the year. It was in March 1973 that the then Governor of Bermuda, Sir Richard Sharples, was murdered together with his aide-de-camp, Captain Hugh Sayers, and his dog while walking in the grounds of his official residence and this subsequently provoked an island-wide riot.

Many members of the Royal Family have visited Government House in Bermuda over the years as it was an ideal stopping-off point when crossing the Atlantic Ocean. One of the first recorded royal guests in Bermuda was Prince Alfred, Duke of Edinburgh, second son of Queen Victoria who landed there in 1861 on a tour that also took in other islands in the Caribbean.

Princess Louise, the fourth daughter of Queen Victoria, stayed in Bermuda for an extended period in 1883 en route to Canada, where her husband was to serve as the Governor-General of Canada. The warm climate was said to suit the Princess and two large hotels on the island were named 'The Princess Hotels' in her honour.

The Prince of Wales (later King Edward VIII) was to pay several visits to Bermuda when he stayed at Government House. The first time was in 1920 and he also returned in 1940 en route to become Governor of The Bahamas. His brother, Prince George, Duke of Kent, visited

Left: A Bermudan postage stamp dating from around 1962, featuring Queen Elizabeth II against a background image of Government House.

Christian Kjelgaard

Bermuda in 1935 on the last stop of his honeymoon with his new wife, Princess Marina, Duchess of Kent.

Queen Elizabeth II went to Bermuda for the first time just six months after her Coronation when she arrived by airplane in November 1953 with the Duke of Edinburgh at the start of their epic six-month Commonwealth tour. Their whirlwind trip to Bermuda included visits to a local airbase, a parade through Hamilton and time spent at the Parliament of Bermuda before they flew on to Jamaica. The Queen and the Duke of Edinburgh would return to Bermuda in 1975 and again in 1994, before their final visit in November 2009, to commemorate Bermuda's 400th anniversary when they stayed again at Government House.

Government House today is used for national and ceremonial functions in Bermuda, as well as receptions and meetings with foreign dignitaries and heads of state. The grounds are opened at specific times of the year, and tourists and locals can once again enjoy the beautifully landscaped gardens.

Bermuda News Bureau, 1953

Right: Queen Elizabeth II planted a tree in the grounds of Government House during her visit in November 1953 at the start of the six-month Commonwealth tour.

Bermuda

Mauritius Images GmbH/Alamy KKRCG9

Government House, Virgin Islands

The Virgin Islands (previously the British Virgin Islands and sometimes known as BVI) are a British Overseas Territory located in the north-eastern Caribbean, comprising 32 small islands and 17 cays. The island archipelago has a total population of about 30,000 people and the capital is Road Town on Tortola, the largest island.

The Virgin Islands, like many islands in the Caribbean, were settled by the Taino, and later the Arawak peoples from South America, who were then displaced by the Caribs. It is said that the first sighting of the Virgin Islands was by explorer Christopher Columbus in 1493, on his second voyage to the Americas.

During the 16th and 17th centuries, European settlers from England, Wales, France, Spain, the Netherlands and Denmark fought for control of the islands. In the 1670s, the British took away control of most of them, including the main island of Tortola, from the Dutch, while the Danish controlled the nearby islands of St Thomas, St John and St Croix. The islands became a key outpost of the sugar trade in the 18th century, with many people brought from Africa to the islands through slavery.

Old Government House BVI Museum website image 7135715

In 1917, the United States purchased the islands controlled by Denmark and renamed them the United States Virgin Islands, with the remaining islands becoming the British Virgin Islands.

In the 19th and 20th centuries, the British

Left: An aerial photograph showing the former residence, Old Government House, on the right and the new Government House, today's official residence of the Governor of the Virgin Islands, on the left.

Opposite page above and images on this page: The Old Government House played an important part in the islands' history as the official residence of the Governor and it hosted many royal visits. It was later transformed into a museum and today is one of the most popular tourist attractions on the islands.

Old Government House BVI Museum website image 343580

Virgin Islands were administered as part of the British Leeward Islands along with nearby St Kitts and Nevis, with an Administrator representing the British Crown and government on the islands. The Virgin Islands became a British Overseas Territory in 1967 and focused their economy on tourism and financial services.

The Governor of the Virgin Islands has been the monarch's representative since 1971 and has an official office at Government House. There have been two houses on the same site in Road Town over the years, being occupied by successive Administrators and Governors. The original residence dating from at least 1887 was initally called Cameron Lodge, and it was built by Sir Edward John Cameron, the first person to be given the title of Administrator of the British Virgin Islands, although the role was sometimes known as the President of the Virgin Islands. In a long career as a diplomat, Sir Edward John Cameron also went on to serve as the colonial Vice-Regal representative in the Leeward Islands, the Turks and Caicos Islands, St Vincent and the Grenadines, the Windward Islands, St Lucia and finally as the Governor of The Gambia until his retirement in 1920.

Government House in the Virgin Islands was built on land that was owned by the family of Sir Edward John Cameron's wife, Eva Selwyn Isaacs, through their connection to the plantation era in the region. Cameron Lodge was constructed on the site of an old military barracks overlooking the main harbour.

Old Government House BVI Museum website images 7152979 7359979

Virgin Islands

When the Cameron family left the islands, the house was sold to the British Foreign Office to be used officially as Government House for the subsequent Administrators and later Governors of the British Virgin Islands. Unfortunately, the house was almost completely destroyed in a violent hurricane in 1924, which left only two rooms intact and large parts of the island uninhabitable. Between 1924 and 1926, work was undertaken to build a new Government House on the site of the destroyed property. The large residence became the focus for official life in the islands and the spacious first-floor sitting room opening onto a sizable verandah enjoyed one of the best views of the capital. The annual garden party at Government House to celebrate the monarch's birthday has entertained hundreds of local citizens.

Today known as 'Old Government House', the residence played an important part in the islands' history and hosted many royal visitors including Queen Elizabeth the Queen Mother and Princess Alice, Countess of Athlone on separate visits in 1964, Queen Elizabeth II in 1966 and again in 1977 (when The Queen arrived on the Royal Yacht *Britannia* as part of her Silver Jubilee tour of the Caribbean), Princess Margaret in 1972, Princess Alexandra in 1988 and Prince Philip, Duke of Edinburgh, in 1994. Prince Charles had lunch at Old Government House in 1972, while the naval ship on which he was serving was at anchor in the main harbour.

Unfortunately, this 1920s property suffered from ongoing damage due to the sub-tropical climate of the region, and the building fell into disrepair. It was closed for renovations in 1996, when the Governor moved temporarily to a private residence on nearby Beef Island. Prince Andrew, Duke of York, was received by the Governor at this location during an official visit in 2000.

There was much debate on the islands about the proposed demolition of the historic building and, after a long campaign, the original house was saved and transformed into a museum as the Old Government House Museum, which opened to the public in 2002. The museum was renovated with the help of volunteers and now features an exhibition about the history of the Virgin Islands and also the Stamp Room, a remarkable philatelic collection of Virgin Islands stamps and postal history.

In 2003, a new Government House was built on land adjacent to the old residence on Tortola. In addition, a new reception hall for official functions held by the Governor was constructed, as well as a courtyard area with panoramic views of the harbour. Today's Government House sits in landscaped gardens with a tennis court and swimming pool. The main residence has five bedrooms and a stylish dining room for formal dinners with a large covered verandah, typical of the elegant houses in the Caribbean. In 2012, the Duke of Gloucester arrived on a four-day visit to the Virgin Islands to mark The Queen's Diamond Jubilee, during which he stayed at Government House. In November 2017, the Prince of Wales paid his second visit to the Virgin Islands to see for himself the devastation caused by Hurricanes Irma and Maria. Unfortunately, the Old Government House Museum experienced significant damage to its historic rooms and furniture inflicted by Hurricane Irma. Prince Charles went to affected areas of Tortola before attending a community reception at Government House for many of those who had assisted with the islands' emergency response to the hurricanes.

Left: The new Government House was built on land adjacent to the old residence in Tortola in 2003.

Old Government House BVI Museum website image 543580

Virgin Islands

Government House, Cayman Islands

The Cayman Islands is a British Overseas Territory in the western Caribbean Sea with a population of just over 65,000 people. The 102 square mile (264 square kilometre) territory is made up of the three islands of Grand Cayman, Cayman Brac and Little Cayman. It is considered to be one of the world's leading offshore financial centres and its capital is George Town.

The islands were largely uninhabited until the 17th century when early European settlers arrived. The Treaty of Madrid gave the British control of both Jamaica and the Cayman Islands in 1670, with a permanent settlement in the latter being established in the 1730s. Records show that the first land grant on the Cayman Islands took place in 1735.

The Cayman Islands came under the jurisdiction of the Governor of Jamaica until 1962, when Jamaica became an independent Commonwealth realm and the Cayman Islands became a British Overseas Territory. The Cayman Islands had a series of Commissioners and Administrators until the post of Governor was established in 1971.

Government House in the Cayman Islands is the official residence of the Governor, the representative of the British monarch and the de facto head of state in the Cayman Islands today. The property is located on Seven Mile Beach in Grand Cayman, reputed to be one of the most beautiful beaches in the world and a major tourist attraction for the islands.

The current Government House was constructed in 1964 as a formal home for the Vice-Regal representative shortly after the Cayman Islands became independent from its near neighbour Jamaica. The property was built as a replacement for a previous official residence and government offices dating from 1907, which were located in George Town and had subsequently been destroyed by fire in 1972. The layout of the new Government House was said to be based on the architectural design for a District Commissioner's house in Nigeria. Government House is a modern building with large landscaped gardens and a beach house that overlooks the public Governor's Beach, a section of the famous Seven Mile Beach.

The present Government House became the full-time official residence of the Governor, whilst a permanent office building, the Government Administration Building (better known locally as the 'Glass House') was built between 1973 and 1975 to accommodate the Governor's Office and the main departments of the Cayman Islands Government.

Cayman Islands

Today, Government House is used for the Cayman Islands' national and ceremonial events. Queen Elizabeth II, as the head of state of the Cayman Islands, together with Prince Philip, Duke of Edinburgh, has visited the islands twice in 1983 and 1994.

Other royal visitors have included Princess Alexandra in 1988 and the Duke of York in 2000. More recently, Prince Edward, Earl of Wessex, and Sophie, Countess of Wessex, went to the islands in March 2016 when they travelled to one of the Cayman Islands smaller islands, Little Cayman, to visit the Central Caribbean Marine Institute. Prince Edward also attended a Duke of Edinburgh's Award Scheme event at Government House on Grand Cayman, while the Countess of Wessex addressed a '100 Women in Hedge Funds' event at the National Gallery in Grand Cayman.

In 2019, the Prince of Wales and the Duchess of Cornwall were welcomed to Government House in the Cayman Islands during a tour that also included both Cayman Brac and Little Cayman. The royal couple inaugurated a new terminal at Owen Roberts International Airport in Grand Cayman, opened a new swimming pool and visited local schools during their two-day visit.

Left: The stretch of Seven Mile Beach in Grand Cayman located to the rear of Government House is known locally as 'The Governor's Beach'.

Cayman Islands

Jack Salen

Government House, Falkland Islands

The Falkland Islands is a British Overseas Territory located in the South Atlantic Ocean, about 300 miles (483 kilometres) east of South America's Patagonian coastline. The archipelago covers an area of 4,700 square miles (12,175 square kilometres) and is made up of the two main islands of East Falkland and West Falkland, with 776 smaller islands. The islands have a combined population of around 4,000 people. The British monarch is represented in the Falkland Islands by the Governor. The Governor of the Falkland Islands is also the Commissioner of South Georgia and the South Sandwich Islands, another British Overseas Territory, with no permanent population that is located about 800 miles (1,290 kilometres) further south in Antarctica in the South Atlantic Ocean.

The Falkland Islands were believed to have been named by Captain John Strong, who led an English expedition which landed on the islands in 1690 and named the islands after his benefactor, Anthony Cary, Viscount Falkland, who was the Treasurer of the Royal Navy at the time. However, the term Falklands Islands was not used until around 1765 when a subsequent expedition arrived in the islands. The islands were settled by European explorers in the 18th century, with the establishment of Port Louis by the French and Port Egmont by the English. After this, the Spanish also arrived and there followed many years of dispute between the rival nations, although the islands remained largely uninhabited.

The British reasserted their sovereignty of the Falkland Islands in 1833, although this action was disputed by Argentina who claimed the islands as part of their territory. In 1840, the Falkland Islands became a Crown colony and settlers from Scotland and Wales established a community there with Port Stanley as the capital. The contested claims over the Falkland Islands continued into the 20th century between the United Kingdom and Argentina, and when Argentinian military invaded the islands in April 1982, the result was an armed conflict between the two countries. The Falkland Islands were restored to British administration two months later, but their sovereign status is still the subject of an ongoing dispute between both nations.

Government House is situated in the Falkland Islands' capital of Stanley, on East Falkland, and it was built in 1845. A large, stone-built house with a slate roof, it is said to be a similar

Falkland Islands

style to a traditional residence found in the islands of Shetland or Orkney, north of Scotland. According to a plaque outside the property to mark the 150th anniversary of the establishment of Stanley in 1994, the original design of Government House was prepared by Richard Clement Moody, the first Governor of the Falkland Islands (1842–1848). The residence has been added to several times over the years and is today used as the home of the Governor, staff offices and for official functions hosted on the islands.

Above: Government House in the Falkland Islands is one of the most remote and southerly of all the official Vice-Regal residences in the Commonwealth.

The famous explorer, Sir Ernest Shackleton, stayed at Government House in the Falkland Islands during one of his famous Antarctic expeditions in the early 20th century. The building was also the site of a major battle during the Argentine invasion of the Falkland Islands in 1982.

The British Royal Family have made several visits to the Falkland Islands over the years. One of the earliest royal visitors was Prince Alfred, Duke of Edinburgh, whose ship, HMS *Galatea* called into the Falkland Islands in 1871, on a return voyage from New Zealand. Some years later in 1957, Prince Philip, Duke of Edinburgh, travelled to the Falkland Islands as part of a voyage to the South Atlantic Ocean on the Royal Yacht *Britannia*. Prince Philip returned to the islands again in 1991. In 1999, the Prince of Wales visited the Falkland Islands, following a six-day visit to Argentina and Uruguay. Prince Charles spent several days on the islands and met different communities during his stay.

A number of royal visits have had military connections especially as the islands have a large Royal Air Force base. The Duke of York has close connections to the Falkland Islands as he fought as a Royal Navy helicopter pilot during the military conflict in 1982 and he has returned to the islands several times. Prince Andrew is also Patron of a number of charities connected to the Falkland Islands. The Duke of Cambridge spent time based at the RAF Mount Pleasant base as a pilot of a search and rescue helicopter in 2012. Although his stay was an unofficial visit, Prince William met many local residents during visits to Stanley.

Below: Government House is the official residence of the Governor of the Falkland Islands and was built in 1845.

A frequent royal visitor to the Falkland Islands has been the Princess Royal, most recently in 2016. During her stay in Stanley, the Princess Royal visited the town's historic Dockyard and Museum, and the King Edward VII Memorial Hospital Day Centre as well as unveiling a Commonwealth Walkway marker. The Princess Royal, accompanied by her husband, Vice-Admiral Sir Timothy Laurence, also paid her first official visit to South Georgia and the South Sandwich Islands to mark the 100th anniversary of Shackleton's 'Endurance' expedition and to see the work of British scientists in the remote islands.

Falkland Islands

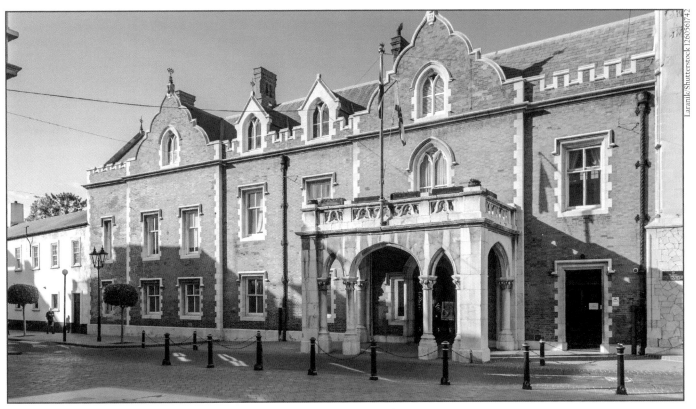

The Convent, Gibraltar

Gibraltar is one of the smallest of the British Overseas Territories, located at the southern tip of the Iberian Peninsula and bordered by Spain to the north. The landscape of 2.5 square miles (6.5 square kilometres) is dominated by the Rock of Gibraltar and a densely populated city area which is home to approximately 30,000 people. The sovereignty of Gibraltar is a major point of contention in Anglo-Spanish relations as Spain asserts a claim to the territory although it was ceded to Great Britain 'in perpetuity' under the Treaty of Utrecht in 1713. During the Second World War, Gibraltar was an important base for the British Royal Navy as it overlooked the entrance to the Mediterranean Sea, which is only around 8 miles (13 kilometres) wide at this point.

In Gibraltar, the Crown is represented by the Governor of Gibraltar, who is appointed by the monarch on the advice of the British Government. The role of the Governor is to act as the de facto head of state and be responsible for formally appointing the Chief Minister of Gibraltar. The Governor is also the Commander-in-Chief of Gibraltar's military forces and has responsibility for defence and security.

Government House, more commonly known as The Convent, has been the official residence of the Governor of Gibraltar since 1728. It was originally a convent of Franciscan friars, hence its name, and it was built in around 1531. After Gibraltar became a British territory in 1713, the Franciscan friary was taken over as the residence of the Governors in 1728 and has remained so ever since. The building was heavily rebuilt during the 18th and 19th centuries in the Georgian style with Victorian elements, but there are many features of its ecclesiastical past that remain.

Image: A. W. Pitaluga/Gibraltar Archivist and licensed by the Gibraltar National Archives of Her Majesty's Government of Gibraltar

Gibraltar

Queen Victoria's father, Prince Edward, Duke of Kent, was appointed as the Governor of Gibraltar in 1802, occupying The Convent as his official residence, but his time in the territory was short-lived and his harsh discipline resulted in a mutiny by the local troops. Although he retained the title of Governor until his death in 1820, he returned to London and was refused permission to return to the territory.

King Edward VII visited Gibraltar in 1903 in the Royal Yacht *Victoria and Albert*. As the first British monarch to set foot in the territory and to inaugurate the new harbour that was being named after the King, there were complaints that as the Supreme Governor of the Church of England, he would be staying in a former Roman Catholic priory. It was noted that the King requested that the residence was referred to only as Government House throughout his time in Gibraltar, with no mention of its ecclesiastical past.

The Convent is situated towards the southern end of Main Street in Gibraltar and its dining room has one of the most extensive displays of heraldry in the Commonwealth, which hang under a vaulted wooden ceiling. Its official rooms include a large hall with portraits of past monarchs. The open-cloistered courtyard of The Convent is used regularly for formal receptions and events which benefit from the usually hot and sunny Mediterranean weather.

The 16th-century garrison church adjacent to The Convent, which was part of the original Franciscan priory, was renamed The Queen's Chapel during the reign of Queen Victoria, but it reverted back to its original name of The King's Chapel under subsequent monarchs including Queen Elizabeth II. The chapel was built in the 1530s but came under the jurisdiction of the Church of England in around 1704 and was used as the main church for the British Army based in Gibraltar for a number of years. The chapel features many military memorials and the regimental colours of various regiments of the British Army. A beautiful stained-glass window in tribute to King George VI was installed in 1952 after the chapel was partially damaged when a military ammunition ship in the harbour exploded, causing widespread damage to nearby buildings.

Outside The Convent, soldiers of the Royal Gibraltar Regiment stand proudly on guard several days each week and a ceremony of the Changing of the Guard takes place on key dates during the year. Among some of the trees in the gardens of the official residence are those planted by King Edward VII, the German Emperor Wilhelm II, the Japanese Emperor Hirohito and Queen Elizabeth II.

Due to its location in the Mediterranean Sea, Gibraltar saw many royal visitors en route to overseas tours in the first part of the 20th century and they frequently stayed at The Convent. King George V and Queen Mary visited Gibraltar several times, firstly in 1901 when they were the Duke and Duchess of Cornwall and York and they were on board the HMS *Ophir* on their way to the Southern Hemisphere. The royal couple came

Above right and below: The 16th-century King's Chapel was part of the original Franciscan priory and served as the main church for the British Army based in Gibraltar for many years. Today, the chapel is used by all three armed forces, the Army, Royal Navy and Royal Air Force, and the chapel is open to the public for regular services.

ashore for lunch with the Royal Fusiliers Regiment, a procession through the town and dinner at The Convent. It was also reported that 1,000lbs of meat and 2,000lbs of bread were distributed to the poor in honour of the royal visit. They returned to Gibraltar in 1906 when they were the Prince and Princess of Wales and they were travelling back from a tour of India on HMS *Renown*.

In 1905, Queen Alexandra, the wife of King Edward VII, arrived in Gibraltar with her daughters, Princess Victoria and Princess Charles of Denmark (later Queen Maud of Norway) to be greeted by many of the ships of the Atlantic Fleet who were moored in the harbour at the time. The royal party enjoyed their visit so much that they came back to Gibraltar for an unofficial stop on their return journey from their Mediterranean tour. Queen Alexandra and her daughters had tea at The Convent before visiting the newly opened Military Hospital. The Queen and Princess Victoria returned the following year for another visit. Queen Alexandra's other daughter, the Princess Royal and her husband, the Duke of Fife, came to Gibraltar in 1907 and stayed for an extended visit attending various functions and events while they were there. In 1908, Prince Arthur, Duke of Connaught, accompanied by the Duchess of Connaught and Princess Patricia of Connaught, came to Gibraltar to visit the military and naval bases and stayed at The Convent.

Many foreign royals also visited Gibraltar. Kaiser Wilhelm II of Germany, grandson of Queen Victoria, came to Gibraltar in 1904 and 1905 in his role as a British Field Marshal and in 1910, King Manuel of Portugal, with his mother, Queen Amelia, arrived in Gibraltar on his yacht, *Amelia IV*, when he went into exile as his country became a republic. The Portuguese royal family later set sail for England.

King George V and Queen Mary returned to Gibraltar in January 1912 on the RMS *Medina* on their return from their tour of India for the Delhi Durbar. Their visit to Gibraltar was cut short due to the death of the Duke of Fife, the husband of their daughter, Princess Louise. However, the royal couple did receive a visit from Infante Don Carlos of Spain and King George V presented new colours to the 1st Battalion of the Staffordshire Regiment in the Grand Parade. The future King George VI – as Prince Albert – called in to Gibraltar in 1913, aboard HMS *Collingwood* when he was serving as a sub-lieutenant in the Royal Navy and he had lunch at The Convent with the Governor and his wife. In April 1921, the Crown Prince Hirohito of Japan visited Gibraltar en route to England. In 1921–22, the Prince of Wales (later King Edward VIII) undertook an eight-month tour of Central Asia and the Far East on HMS *Renown* and he visited Gibraltar on the outward and return journeys. The Prince came to The Convent for several dinners and a garden party.

In 1954, Gibraltar welcomed Queen Elizabeth II and the Duke of Edinburgh on their return from their six-month tour of Commonwealth nations in the Southern Hemisphere. The Queen's young children, Prince Charles and Princess Anne, travelled out to Gibraltar to meet their parents and went back to London with them on board the Royal Yacht *Britannia*. In 1981, Prince Charles returned to Gibraltar with Princess Diana to board the Royal Yacht *Britannia* for their honeymoon, which caused some controversy in Spain and prevented the Spanish King and Queen from attending their wedding in London.

Since then, royal visits to Gibraltar have been much rarer as diplomatic relations with Spain have been carefully managed. The Princess Royal visited Gibraltar in 2004 to mark the 300th anniversary of British settlement in Gibraltar and she returned in 2009 for a three-day visit to inaugurate the Princess Royal Medical Centre and to tour the Royal Naval base. In 2012, Prince Edward, the Earl of Wessex and Sophie, Countess of Wessex, were welcomed to Gibraltar with a parade and huge crowds in Main Street for a three-day visit to mark the Diamond Jubilee of Queen Elizabeth II.

Gibraltar

Ross Barclay

Government House, Montserrat

Montserrat is a small 39 square mile (101 square kilometre) British Overseas Territory in the north-east Caribbean with a small population of around 5,000 permanent residents. The island was said to have been named by explorer Christopher Columbus in 1493 after the Monastery of Montserrat in Spain and the word 'Montserrat' means 'serrated mountain' in Catalan.

Among the first European settlers to arrive on the island were a group of Irish men in 1632, a fact which is still acknowledged in Montserrat society today with celebrations for St Patrick's Day that also recognise a later uprising by slaves on 17 March 1768, who were brought from Africa to Montserrat to work on plantations. The island came under English control in the 1660s after disputes with the French and its economy grew due to the sugar, rum and cotton trade.

Montserrat was originally one of the Leeward Islands, which was governed as a group of islands from 1871 to 1958 before each of them became independent. Montserrat was part of the short-lived West Indies Federation from 1958 to 1962, before it became a British Overseas Territory with its own Governor from 1971.

Ross Barclay

The island's recent history has been dominated by the eruptions of the previously dormant Soufrière Hills volcano between 1995 and 1999, which destroyed Montserrat's Georgian-era capital of Plymouth and the small airport, and caused two-thirds of the island's population to flee. An exclusion zone remains in place across much of Montserrat today and the centre of government and business moved to Brades in the north as people gradually returned to the island.

Above left and left: The original Government House in Montserrat, dating from the late 19th century, pictured in 1991 before the official residence had to be abandoned due to damage caused by the volcanic activity on the island.

Right: The original Government House pictured before it was abandoned following volcanic activity on the island.

Ross Barclay

The original Government House in Montserrat was built for the Governor of the Leeward Islands, who was ordinarily resident in Antigua and used the house in Montserrat during official visits there. The property dates from the late 19th century and is located in Plymouth in the south of the island. The two-storey colonial-era residence had to be abandoned due to structural damage and the ongoing volcanic activity within the exclusion zone. The shell of the original house exists but is inaccessible to all residents.

A new modern Government House was established in extensive gardens at Woodlands as the formal home of the Governor of Montserrat and is used for the majority of official functions on the island.

Queen Elizabeth II and the Duke of Edinburgh went to Montserrat during a tour of the Caribbean in February 1966. Since then, several members of the Royal Family have visited the island to see the devastation caused by the volcano including Prince Andrew, Duke of York, who visited a number of times in the late 1990s; the Prince of Wales and the Duchess of Cornwall, who arrived in Montserrat for a short visit in 2008; and Prince Edward, Earl of Wessex, and Sophie, Countess of Wessex, who represented The Queen on their 2012 Diamond Jubilee visit.

Below: Much of the south of the island of Montserrat had to be abandoned in the 1990s due the ongoing volcanic activity within the exclusion zone. The original Government House of Montserrat (circled) can be seen in this photograph near to the abandoned town of Plymouth.

Derek Galon/iStock 830509596

Montserrat

Plantation House, St Helena

The islands of St Helena, Ascension and Tristan da Cunha are collectively a British Overseas Territory on a series of small, volcanic, tropical islands in the South Atlantic Ocean. One of the remotest territories in the Commonwealth, St Helena and Tristan da Cunha until recently were only accessible by ship before a new airport was opened in St Helena in 2016. The most populated island at just under 5,000 people, St Helena is the administrative centre of the Overseas Territory and the Governor of St Helena is the British monarch's representative across the islands, although there are separate Administrator positions on both Ascension and Tristan da Cunha. A small Government House exists in Ascension Island, but this is an administrative office building rather than the official residence of the Administrator, which is located at The Residency in Ascension Island.

The history of St Helena is said to have begun in the early 1500s, when Spanish and Portuguese explorers first located the islands. It is widely accepted that St Helena was first discovered on 21 May 1502 by the Galician explorer, João da Nova, on behalf of the King of Portugal. It is said that he named the island, St Helena, after St Helena of Constantinople, whose Saints Day falls on that date although this is disputed by some historians.

The English began to use the islands as a base to attack passing Spanish, Portuguese and Dutch ships, and in 1657 Oliver Cromwell granted the East India Company, the governorship of St Helena. The island's royal charter was granted after the restoration of the monarchy in 1660 and its capital was established at Jamestown, named in honour of James, Duke of York (later King James II of England). In 1815, the British government selected St Helena as the place of detention for Napoleon Bonaparte, who arrived in October of that year with a battalion of soldiers to guard him. Although officially under detention, Napoleon had an official residence at Longwood House, where he died on 5 May 1821. The house where Napoleon passed away remains French property, under the authority of the French Ministry of Foreign Affairs.

Above: Plantation House in St Helena is the home to several of the world's oldest living tortoises including Jonathan, who at the grand age of 187, continues to live in the gardens.

Meenakshi Dhar

Plantation House is the official residence of the Governor of St Helena and it is located to the south of the capital, Jamestown in a beautiful valley. The property was built in around 1791–92 by the East India Company when the company governed the island before it became a Crown Colony. The house was initially chosen as a 'summer' home for the Governor, while the main administration of St Helena was undertaken from The Castle, the Governor's town residence in Jamestown. The plantation role of the house, supplying goods and farm produce for the Governor and his staff, gave the building its name.

The house was extended in 1816 with some further additions in the 1960s, but the main features of the impressive colonial-style residence remain largely unchanged. It has 35 rooms, including the large reception room displaying portraits of British monarchs. The formal dining room seats more than 20 people for dinner and features a portrait of the Duke of Wellington, who stayed at the property in 1805 on his way back from India. The library, which contains around 2,000 books, was one of the original rooms built in 1816 and many pieces of 18th-century and Regency furniture and porcelain can be found in the house.

Most of the rooms in Plantation House have brass plaques on the doors, recording the original purpose of the quarters. Names include the Governor's Room, Admiral's Room, General's Room and Baron's Room. Legend also has it that there was also a 'Prince of Orange Bedroom', named after the 1838 visit of Prince William Henry Frederick of Orange from the Netherlands, but it is not recorded which room he is supposed to have stayed in.

The roof was originally slate but was replaced with a metal roof like most properties on the island. Previous Governors and their families have faced considerable problems with the house, including a period of stagnant water that caused typhoid in the 19th century and termites (white ants) infesting the property several times in the early 20th century.

Plantation House contains a rare vellum-bound book called 'Plantation Notes' that was first used in 1891 by Governor Grey Wilson to record significant changes to the house and grounds for the benefit of future Governors. It contains a wealth of information and has

David Stanley

Above right and right:
Plantation House dates
from around 1791–92 and is
the official residence of the
Governor of St Helena.

St Helena

David Stanley

Left: The entrance hall at Plantation House features many fine portraits and paintings.

been continuously used, except from the mid-1930s to the mid-1950s when the book was lost for a couple of decades before being rediscovered at The Castle archives.

Plantation House is designated as a Grade I listed building today and is not generally open to the public, although guided tours can be requested with the Governor's Office. The grounds of over 100-acres (40-hectares) are home to several of the world's oldest living tortoises including Jonathan, who at the grand age of 187, continues to live in the gardens of Plantation House with five other giant tortoises. The grounds also feature the remains of the 'Ladies Bath', a small outdoor pool used by the women of the residence, and many rare species of plants and flowers from the island.

Many illustrious people came to St Helena over the centuries, including Charles Darwin, Rudyard Kipling and Winston Churchill, and they were often entertained at Plantation House. The first royal visit to St Helena was Prince Rupert, the nephew of King Charles I, who anchored in Rupert's Bay in the 17th century, giving the bay its name. One of the first official royal visitors to St Helena to go to Plantation House was Prince Alfred, later Duke of Edinburgh, in 1860 when he was serving on the Royal Navy's ship HMS *Euryalus*; he dined at Plantation House and attended a ball in his honour at The Castle.

The Duke and Duchess of Connaught and Strathearn visited Plantation House in 1910 with their daughter, Princess Patricia of Connaught, whose signed portrait hangs in the entrance hall. The royal party arrived on HMS

David Stanley

Left: Longwood House was the official residence of Napoleon Bonaparte during his exile and detention in St Helena. The house remains the property of the French Government today.

David Stanley

Above: The formal dining room seats more than 20 people for dinner and features a portrait of the Duke of Wellington, who stayed at the property in 1805.

Balmoral Castle on their way to South Africa to open the first Parliament of the Union of South Africa and they were met by the Governor of St Helena before visiting The Castle, the hospital, the lace school and a flax mill.

The Prince of Wales (later King Edward VIII) was welcomed to Plantation House in August 1925, when he stayed on the island for two days to fulfil a busy programme of engagements. The Prince arrived on HMS *Repulse*, the largest ship to have visited St Helena to that date, and also took a great interest in the visit to Longwood House and Napoleon's Tomb, where he planted a tree to mark his visit, before attending a formal dance at Plantation House.

The first and only visit by a reigning monarch to St Helena was on 29 April 1947, when King George VI with Queen Elizabeth and the young Princesses Elizabeth and Margaret came ashore from HMS *Vanguard*, following their successful tour of South Africa. There was doubt that the Princesses would visit the island as they were said to be suffering from heavy colds, but they accompanied their parents at the last minute. After a carriage tour of St Helena and a trip to Napoleon's former residence at Longwood House, the royal party visited Plantation House for tea where they met the famous tortoises in its grounds.

The Duke of Edinburgh visited St Helena in 1957, travelling on the newly commissioned Royal Yacht *Britannia* and planted a cypress tree in the grounds of Plantation House before attending a lunch and garden party. The Duke visited the local hospital, a flax mill and was presented with a lace table set as a gift for The Queen. He also opened the new playground for children in Jamestown which was known as the 'Duke of Edinburgh Playground'.

Prince Andrew visited St Helena in 1984 when he was a serving naval officer on HMS *Herald*. During his short visit, he attended a number of events including a dance and musical performance. In honour of his visit, the island's new secondary school was named after him when it opened in 1989.

The most recent royal visitor to St Helena was the Princess Royal in 2002 when she came to mark the quincentenary of the discovery of the island. The Princess arrived on the RMS *St Helena* and during her first day on the island attended a parade in Jamestown before visiting the museum and the local hospital. She later dedicated the foundation stone for the Princess Royal Community Care Centre and attended a formal dinner at Plantation House where she was staying. On her second day, the Princess Royal was given a tour of the Napoleonic sites on the island by the Honorary French Consul before visiting Longwood House; this was followed by a visit to the Levelwood Community Centre to meet senior citizens, lunch with students from the Prince Andrew School Council, a visit to an agricultural show and a school concert. On her final day, the Princess attended a service at the St Helena Cathedral before departing by ship.

St Helena

Waterloo, Turks and Caicos

The Turks and Caicos Islands are a British Overseas Territory consisting of the larger Caicos Islands and smaller Turks Islands in the northern Caribbean. The islands cover over 170 square miles (430 square kilometres) and the resident population is just over 37,000 people. Cockburn Town, the capital since 1766, is situated on Grand Turk Island.

The official residence of the Governor is located on Grand Turk, and it was named Waterloo after the famous Napoleonic battle of the same name fought in 1815, the same year that the property was built. Its design is in the traditional Bermudan style, with one wing and an open-air kitchen, characteristic of the Caribbean region at the time.

In 1857, James Misick, the owner of Waterloo, sold the property for £1,046 to the British Government as they had been looking for a residence for the Crown's Vice-Regal representative in the Turks and Caicos Islands, then known as the President. In 1873, the islands became a dependency of Jamaica at the request of the local people and the monarch was no longer represented by a President but by a Commissioner, who reported to the Governor of Jamaica, and who lived at Waterloo.

Above and below: Waterloo features lots of commemorative items and photographs from the many Governors who have stayed at the residence.

After Jamaica became independent in 1962, responsibility for the Turks and Caicos Islands fell to the Governor of The Bahamas, who nominated Administrators to represent the Crown there and they continued to live at Waterloo. However, when The Bahamas gained independence in 1973, the islands received their own Governor and have remained a separate autonomous British Overseas Territory ever since.

All images: Andrew Mann

All images: Andrew Mann

Above: Waterloo was named after the famous Napoleonic battle as the property was constructed in 1815.

The smaller island of Salt Cay, which was the main location for the salt and brine industry that helped the islands to develop in the 19th century, is also the location for a former Vice-Regal residence known today as Old Government House, Salt Cay, although it has previously been known as the Old Commissioner's House and the Government Guest House. This building is said to date from 1795 and was a secondary home for the local Commissioner of the islands when they would oversee the local industry. It is now part of a local National Trust project to restore the historical ruin back to its former glory.

Today, the Governor's Office at Waterloo is one of the most important historical buildings in the Turks and Caicos Islands. It is fortunate that the residence has been well cared for, and has survived fires, termites, remodelling work and hurricanes in 1866, 1926, 1945 and 2008. Renovations and improvements to Waterloo were commissioned in 1993, to restore as far as possible the original features, including the windows and the property's unusual guttering. A nine-hole golf course was created in the grounds in 1999 that is still used by local players.

The house is regularly used for official meetings between the Governor and the Premier or the official opposition and local community groups, and school children are often invited to tour the property.

The first official royal visit to Turks and Caicos took place in 1960 by Princess Mary, the Princess Royal, who arrived on the Royal Yacht *Britannia* for an extensive stay. Other royal visitors have included Queen Elizabeth II and the Duke of Edinburgh in 1966, Princess Alexandra in 1988 and Prince Andrew in 2000.

Turks and Caicos

Government Houses: References, Websites and Source Notes:

General:
- Wikipedia – Government Houses of the Commonwealth: www.wikipedia.org
- Website of the British Monarchy: www.royal.uk
- *Royal Lives: Portraits of Past Royals by those in the know*, (eds.) Brian Harrison and Frank Prochaska (OUP, 2002)
- *Intimate Portraits of Kings, Queens and Courtiers*, by Kenneth Rose (Spring Books, 1985)
- *The Royal Encyclopedia*, (eds.) Edited by Ronald Allison and Sarah Riddell (Macmillan Press, 1991)

Antigua and Barbuda:
- *The History of Government House*, Dr Reginald Murphy (GOH, 2016)

Australia:
- Governor-General of Australia official website - Government House and Admiralty House: www.gg.gov.au
- *The Memoirs of Princess Alice, Duchess of Gloucester*, Princess Alice (Collins, 1983)
- Government House, New South Wales: www.governor.nsw.gov.au/government-house/
- Government House, Victoria: www.governor.vic.gov.au/history
- Government House, Queensland: www.govhouse.qld.gov.au/government-house.aspx
- *Government House, Queensland*, (guidebook first published in 2012 and reprinted in 2015)
- *Government House and Western Australian Society 1829-2010*, Dr Jeremy C. Martens (UWA Press, 2011)
- *Government House, Western Australia*, Heritage Perth website: http://heritageperth.com.au/properties/government-house/
- Government House, Western Australia: www.govhouse.wa.gov.au
- Government House, South Australia: www.governor.sa.gov.au
- Government House, Tasmania: www.govhouse.tas.gov.au
- *Government House, Tasmania Open House* (booklet, 2015)
- Government House, Northern Territory: www.govhouse.nt.gov.au
- *Government House Northern Territory* (official brochure and history of GH, 2014)
- *Government House, Norfolk Island* (guidebook, 2013)
- Government House, Norfolk Island, Burnt Pine Travel: www.burntpinetravel.com/norfolk-island/world-heritage-area

The Bahamas:
- Bahamas website: www.bahamas.com/vendor/government-house
- *The Windsor Team* by Janet Flanner, *Life Magazine*, 9 June 1941, page 122
- *Nassau's Historic Buildings*, C. Seighbert Russell (Bahamas National Trust, 1982)

Barbados:
- Barbados tourism website: www.barbados.org/government-house-barbados.htm
- Barbados tourism website: www.gobarbados.org/government-house-barbados

Belize:
- Belize Historical Society Newsletter, Nov/Dec 1995
- *Belize Today* (Volume 1, No. 4), June 1987
- *The New Belize* (Volume XV, No. 10), October 1985

Canada:
- *Rideau Hall: An Illustrated History of Government House, Ottawa*, R. H. Hubbard (McGill/Queen's University Press, 1977)
- Governor-General of Canada official website – Rideau Hall and La Citadelle: www.gg.ca
- *The Governor-General and the Prime Ministers*, Edward McWhinney (Ronsdale Press, 2005)
- *Ample Mansions: The Vice-Regal Residences of the Canadian Provinces*, R. H. Hubbard (University of Ottawa Press, 1989)
- Lieutenant-Governor of Alberta official website: www.lieutenantgovernor.ab.ca/about-the-lieutenant-governor/lieutenant-governor-s-suite
- Alberta's Government House: www.assembly.ab.ca/lao/library/lt-gov/house.html
- Lieutenant-Governor of British Columbia official website: https://ltgov.bc.ca
- Government House, Manitoba official website: www.manitobalg.ca
- Government House, New Brunswick official website: https://www2.gnb.ca/content/gnb/en/lgnb/house.html
- Government House, Newfoundland and Labrador official website: www.govhouse.nl.ca/governmenthouse
- Commissioner of Yukon official website: https://commissionerofyukon.ca
- Commissioner's Residence, Dawson, Parks Canada website: http://www.pc.gc.ca/apps/dfhd/page_fhbro_eng.aspx?id=3032
- Government House, Nova Scotia official website: http://lt.gov.ns.ca/government-house
- *The Romance of Government House: Nova Scotia*, James Stuart Martell (First published in 1939, reprint Dept of Government Services, 1983)
- *Royal Roots: The Crown in Nova Scotia*, Elizabeth Eve (Province of Nova Scotia, 1998)
- Lieutenant-Governor of Ontario official website: www.lgontario.ca
- Government House, Prince Edward Island official website: www.lgpei.ca
- *Government House and the Fanningbank Estate: A Guidebook*, Reginald Porter (2015)
- Lieutenant-Governor of Quebec official website: www.lieutenant-gouverneur.qc.ca
- Government House, Saskatchewan official website: https://governmenthousesk.ca/

Grenada:
- Video: *Government House, Grenada* by Kenrick Fletcher, published on 13 May 2013: https://youtu.be/Ep7oXqhYUEw

Jamaica:
- The Governor-General of Jamaica official website: www.kingshouse.gov.jm
- *History of King's House*, research paper by the Office of the Governor-General (1999, updated 2016)
- *Old King's House, Spanish Town*, booklet published by Old King's House Restoration Fund (1959)

New Zealand:
- Governor-General of New Zealand official website: www.gg.govt.nz/government-house
- *Government House Wellington* (official guidebook, 2002)
- *Government House Wellington* (visitors guide, 2012)
- University of Auckland website, Old Government House: www.auckland.ac.nz/en/about-us/community-services/old-government-house.html

Solomon Islands:
- *Solomon Islands Historical Encyclopaedia, 1893-1978* website: www.solomonencyclopaedia.net/biogs/E000760b.htm

St Lucia:
- Governor-General of St Lucia official website: http://governorgeneral.govt.lc

St Vincent and the Grenadines:
- Government of St Vincent website: www.gov.vc/index.php/history-of-government-house

St Kitts and Nevis:
- Historic St Kitts website: www.historicstkitts.kn/places/government-house
- Governor-General of St Kitts and Nevis official website: www.gg.gov.kn
- Alluring World travel website: www.alluringworld.com/government-house

Tuvalu:
- *Australian Women's Weekly*, 18 October 1978: https://trove.nla.gov.au/newspaper/article/51769724/4772579

Jersey:
- Lieutenant-Governor of Jersey official website: www.governmenthouse.gov.je/governmenthouse/
- *Old Jersey Houses II*, Joan Stevens (Chichester: Pillimore & Co. Ltd. ISBN 0-85033-269-9, 1977)
- The Island Wiki: www.theislandwiki.org/index.php/Government_House

Guernsey:
- Government House, Guernsey official website: www.governmenthouse.gg
- Guernsey Royal Court: http://www.guernseyroyalcourt.gg/article/1944/Royal-Visits-to-the-Bailiwick

- *At Their Majesties' Service*, Colonel Richard Graham (Gateway Publishing, 2014)
- Old Government House Hotel website: www.theoghhotel.com/about/history

Sark:
- La Seigneurie: www.laseigneuriegardens.com

Isle of Man:
- Lieutenant-Governor of Isle of Man: https://www.gov.im/about-the-government/departments/cabinet-office/external-relations/crown-services/office-of-lieutenant-governor/
- *Government Houses in the Isle of Man*, Peter J. Hulme (The Manx Experience in conjunction with the Isle of Man Government, 1990).

Bermuda:
- Government of Bermuda website: www.gov.bm/governor-bermuda
- 'Heritage Matters - 399 years, 120 Governors and five stately mansions' by Dr Edward Harris, *The Royal Gazette*, 12/03/2011: www.royalgazette.com/article/20110312/island09/703129987
- Bermuda Attractions website: www.bermuda-attractions.com/bermuda2_000128.htm
- Video: *Inside Bermuda's Homes – Government House*: https://vimeo.com/179723540

Virgin Islands:
- 'History of Government House British Virgin Islands' by Michael Kent (written for BVI website)
- Old Government House Museum website: www.oghm.org

Cayman Islands:
- National Archives website: http://webarchive.nationalarchives.gov.uk/20130225150739/http://ukincayman.fco.gov.uk/en/about-us/government-house/

Falkland Islands:
- Falkland Islands Tourism: https://www.falklandislands.com/things-to-do/government-house-p673671

Gibraltar:
- *The rock of the Gibraltarians: a history of Gibraltar*, Sir William G. F Jackson (p. 261, 2nd ed., Grendon: Gibraltar Books, 1990, ISBN 0948466146)
- Neville Chipulina Gibraltar Blog: https://gibraltar-social-history.blogspot.com/

St Helena:
- *The History of Plantation House: St Helena*, Lady Margaret Field (Patten Press, 1998, ISBN 1872229328)
- *Plantation House: The Governor's Residence* by Edward Coke: http://sainthelenaisland.info/plantationhouse.htm

Turks and Caicos:
- 'Waterloo is part of Turks and Caicos Islands living history – Governor', *Turks and Caicos Weekly News*, 15 June 2015

Acknowledgements

This book project has taken a number of years and I have been assisted by many contributors across the world.

I have always been interested in British royalty and I have been collecting memorabilia and books, and researching and writing about the Royal Family for many years. In 2004, I embarked on a 'gap year' in Australia and New Zealand, primarily based in Sydney, Australia. I would walk to work through the Botanical Gardens in Sydney Harbour and go past a very grand building that I soon discovered was Government House, New South Wales.

On going inside, I discovered a fascinating world of formal state rooms, that included a throne room and reception rooms. The walls were adorned with portraits of kings and queens, past and present, and I was struck by the fact that, even though I was thousands of miles away from Buckingham Palace, here was a very real and tangible link with the Crown. Government House was the embodiment of the Crown and the monarch in the many realms and dominions of first, the British Empire, and then later, many of the countries of the Commonwealth.

I began to appreciate that Government Houses existed all over the world, in Commonwealth countries and overseas territories. They came in all shapes and sizes, different architectural styles, and they all had one thing in common – their link to the Crown. It started me on a journey of discovery that has resulted in this book of the current Government Houses in the Commonwealth, and I am fortunate that my travels have taken me to visit some (but not all) of these Vice-Regal residences.

I would like to thank the many individuals who have shared their photographs of the various official residences with me, and the photographers – amateur and professional – who have kindly given permission for their images to be published in this book. I would not have been able to complete this project without them.

I would like to thank the many staff members at Government Houses across the Commonwealth who have provided me with information, archive materials, anecdotes and granted permission to publish images from their official websites and archives.

I have also been kindly assisted by many correspondents, contacts, archivists and others with an interest in the Government Houses across the world.

Finally, I would like to thank my partner, my parents, my family, my friends and my work colleagues who have supported me in this project.

About the Author

Jeffrey Hyland is an occasional freelance writer specialising in various subjects such as British royalty, history, travel and London.

Image: Nina Hollington Photography

His work has been published a number of times including in *Majesty Magazine* on the subjects of the Royal Red Cross, Royal University Chancellors and the connections between the City of London Livery Companies and the Royal Family. He has also been published in the *Middle Temple Magazine* on the topic of the 'Royal Benchers of the Inns of Court'.

In his professional life, Jeffrey has many years' experience in Public Relations, Communications and Marketing in both the public and private sectors. His current role is as the Editor of *The Parliamentarian*, the Journal of Commonwealth Parliaments, and as Communications Manager for the Commonwealth Parliamentary Association, a job that has taken him to many Commonwealth countries.

This is his first published book on the current Government Houses across the Commonwealth and he is planning a second title exploring many former and lost Government Houses throughout the world.

To contact Jeffrey Hyland please email: jeffreyalexanderhyland@hotmail.com.

For more information about his work visit: www.jeffreyhyland.wordpress.com

Constance Grace 1921-2019
Special thanks to my 'royal' supporter and Nana Connie who always followed my interest in royalty over the years.